Microsoft Dynamics CRM 2011 Application Design

Develop applications for any situation with our hands-on guide to Microsoft Dynamics CRM 2011

Mahender Pal

PUBLISHING

BIRMINGHAM - MUMBAI

Microsoft Dynamics CRM 2011 Application Design

First published: December 2012

Production Reference: 1131212

Published by Packt Publishing Ltd.
Livery Place
35 Livery Street
Birmingham B3 2PB, UK.

ISBN 978-1-84968-456-9

www.packtpub.com

Cover Image by Javier Barría C. (jbarriac@yahoo.com)

Credits

About the Author

Mahender Pal is a Microsoft Dynamics CRM specialist. He has experience in envisioning and developing xRM solutions and providing consultancy for Microsoft Dynamics CRM, SharePoint, and Silverlight. Currently he is working with Cipher Dynamics IT Services India as CRM Practice Manager.

A Microsoft Most Valuable Professional (MVP) for Dynamics CRM for three years, he loves to contribute to the Dynamics CRM community and has a dedicated personal blog (http://mahenderpal.wordpress.com/) where he contributes various technical articles to assist the Microsoft Dynamics CRM community.

I would like to dedicate this book to my father, the late Mr. Joginder Singh. He had to forgo his school at primary level because of family conditions but worked very hard in life so that he could inculcate strong values and gave utmost importance to education in the lives of his children.

I would like to thank Packt Publishing for giving me the opportunity to write this book, my special thanks to Amey Kanse, Martin Bell, Joel Goveya, and my technical reviewers Nishant Rana and James Wood for giving me their valuable feedback for my drafts.

My special thanks to my wife Sonia, my daughter Diksha, and my son Arnav for supporting me while I was writing this book.

And finally, I would like to thank my friends, my team members Anil Sharma, Vikram Singh, Namita Sethi, Mala Mishra, and Gopinath, my elder brother Jasbir Singh, and Microsoft Dynamics CRM community for their continuous support.

About the Reviewers

Nishant Rana currently works in Microsoft Global Services India. He has been actively involved with .NET since its release. His main focus area has been Microsoft Dynamics CRM and SharePoint. He is a Microsoft Certified Technology Specialist and an IT Professional in Dynamics, SharePoint, and MCAD (Application Developer) for .NET.

You can contact Nishant via his website at http://nishantrana.wordpress.com/ or follow him on Twitter at @nishantranaCRM.

James Wood is a Technical Consultant at 2e2 with skills in the end-to-end implementation of enterprise-level Microsoft Dynamics CRM solutions. He graduated from the University of Huddersfield with a First Class Honors Degree in Computer Games Programming before making the switch to business applications.

He has worked with Microsoft Dynamics CRM for a little under three years. He is also an able developer of bespoke applications, and most recently became an active member of StackOverflow. You can read his blog at www.woodsworkblog.wordpress.com.

His time at 2e2 has cemented his skills in software design and development coupled with an ability to consult with clients to realize their goals. He has worked on a number of medium to large Microsoft Dynamics CRM implementations in sectors including local and regional government, education, defense, banking, manufacturing, and welfare.

I would like to thank my family and friends for everything.

www.PacktPub.com

Support files, eBooks, discount offers and more

You might want to visit www.PacktPub.com for support files and downloads related to your book.

Did you know that Packt offers eBook versions of every book published, with PDF and ePub files available? You can upgrade to the eBook version at www.PacktPub.com and as a print book customer, you are entitled to a discount on the eBook copy. Get in touch with us at service@packtpub.com for more details.

At www.PacktPub.com, you can also read a collection of free technical articles, sign up for a range of free newsletters and receive exclusive discounts and offers on Packt books and eBooks.

http://PacktLib.PacktPub.com

Do you need instant solutions to your IT questions? PacktLib is Packt's online digital book library. Here, you can access, read and search across Packt's entire library of books.

Why Subscribe?

- Fully searchable across every book published by Packt
- Copy and paste, print and bookmark content
- On demand and accessible via web browser

Free Access for Packt account holders

If you have an account with Packt at www.PacktPub.com, you can use this to access PacktLib today and view nine entirely free books. Simply use your login credentials for immediate access.

Instant Updates on New Packt Books

Get notified! Find out when new books are published by following @PacktEnterprise on Twitter, or the *Packt Enterprise* Facebook page.

Table of Contents

Preface

Apart from delivering exciting CRM features, Microsoft CRM 2011 provides a robust xRM Application Framework that can be used to develop different business applications.

In this book, you will learn about the new features introduced in Microsoft CRM 2011. You will also learn about the out-of-box (OOB) features provided by Microsoft CRM 2011 and use them to develop applications for different industries. This book will help you to use Microsoft CRM 2011 processes in real-world applications. You will learn how to customize and extend Microsoft CRM 2011.

You will also learn how to create and deploy Bing maps application in the Silverlight.

What this book covers

Chapter 1, Getting Started with Microsoft Dynamics CRM 2011, will explain the different deployment options and clients for Microsoft CRM 2011. You will learn about the hardware and software requirements for Microsoft CRM 2011.

Chapter 2, Customizing Microsoft Dynamics CRM 2011, will help you to understand customization concepts, e-mail integration, and how to use the marketing module in Microsoft CRM 2011. It will help you to develop Project Training Enrolment System.

Chapter 3, Using Process in Microsoft Dynamics CRM 2011, shows how to use, process, and configure security in Microsoft CRM 2011. This chapter will help you to develop Employee Recruitment Management System.

Chapter 4, Implementing Business Logic through Plugins, will help you to understand plugins in Microsoft CRM 2011. You will learn to use sub-grids, set products, and set a pricelist. It will help you to develop a hotel management application using Microsoft CRM 2011.

Chapter 5, Using Web Resources in Microsoft CRM 2011, will help you to understand, create, and use web resources. In this chapter, you will learn to create the Bing Maps application using Silverlight.

Chapter 6, Using External Web Application in Microsoft CRM 2011, covers application development using Microsoft CRM 2011 web services. You will learn to create and deploy custom editable grid view web applications in Microsoft CRM 2011.

Chapter 7, Using Mobile Client in Microsoft CRM 2011, covers the mobile client for Microsoft CRM 2011.

Chapter 8, Issue Tracker using Microsoft CRM 2011, will help you to learn and create the custom workflow assembly and auto number plugins in Microsoft CRM 2011. This chapter will help you to create the Issue Tracker application using Microsoft CRM 2011.

Appendix A, Data Model, covers the data models for the Account and Contact entities along with their attributes.

Appendix B, Hotel Entity Data Model and Design, covers all the entities and their attributes that we need in the hotel managemnt sysytem.

What you need for this book

You will require the following software products and browsers for this book:

- Windows Internet Explorer 8 or later
- Microsoft .NET Framework 4
- Microsoft Visual Studio 2010
- Microsoft Silverlight Developer Runtime
- Microsoft Silverlight Tools for Visual Studio 2010
- Microsoft Dynamics CRM 2011
- Microsoft SQL Server 2008
- Microsoft Dynamics CRM 2011 E-mail Router
- The latest version of Microsoft Dynamics CRM 2011 SDK
- Plug-in Registration Tool for Microsoft Dynamics CRM 2011
- Developer Extensions for Microsoft Dynamics CRM 2011
- Bing Maps Silverlight Control

Who this book is for

This book has been written for technical consultants working with Microsoft CRM 2011, who want to use Microsoft CRM 2011 as an xRM platform. It is for those who have the knowledge of .NET, JavaScript, and Silverlight.

Conventions

In this book, you will find a number of styles of text that distinguish between different kinds of information. Here are some examples of these styles, and an explanation of their meaning.

Code words in text are shown as follows: "We can include other contexts through the use of the include directive."

A block of code is set as follows:

```
[default]
exten => s,1,Dial(Zap/1|30)
exten => s,2,Voicemail(u100)
exten => s,102,Voicemail(b100)
exten => i,1,Voicemail(s0)
```

When we wish to draw your attention to a particular part of a code block, the relevant lines or items are set in bold:

```
[default]
exten => s,1,Dial(Zap/1|30)
exten => s,2,Voicemail(u100)
exten => s,102,Voicemail(b100)
exten => i,1,Voicemail(s0)
```

Any command-line input or output is written as follows:

```
# cp /usr/src/asterisk-addons/configs/cdr_mysql.conf.sample
    /etc/asterisk/cdr_mysql.conf
```

New terms and **important words** are shown in bold. Words that you see on the screen, in menus or dialog boxes for example, appear in the text like this: "clicking the **Next** button moves you to the next screen".

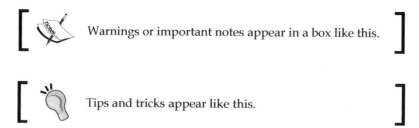

Warnings or important notes appear in a box like this.

Tips and tricks appear like this.

Reader feedback

Feedback from our readers is always welcome. Let us know what you think about this book—what you liked or may have disliked. Reader feedback is important for us to develop titles that you really get the most out of.

To send us general feedback, simply send an e-mail to feedback@packtpub.com, and mention the book title via the subject of your message.

If there is a topic that you have expertise in and you are interested in either writing or contributing to a book, see our author guide on www.packtpub.com/authors.

Customer support

Now that you are the proud owner of a Packt book, we have a number of things to help you to get the most from your purchase.

Downloading the example code

You can download the example code files for all Packt books you have purchased from your account at http://www.PacktPub.com. If you purchased this book elsewhere, you can visit http://www.PacktPub.com/support and register to have the files e-mailed directly to you.

Errata

Although we have taken every care to ensure the accuracy of our content, mistakes do happen. If you find a mistake in one of our books—maybe a mistake in the text or the code—we would be grateful if you would report this to us. By doing so, you can save other readers from frustration and help us improve subsequent versions of this book. If you find any errata, please report them by visiting http://www.packtpub. com/support, selecting your book, clicking on the **errata submission form** link, and entering the details of your errata. Once your errata are verified, your submission will be accepted and the errata will be uploaded on our website, or added to any list of existing errata, under the Errata section of that title. Any existing errata can be viewed by selecting your title from http://www.packtpub.com/support.

Piracy

Piracy of copyright material on the Internet is an ongoing problem across all media. At Packt, we take the protection of our copyright and licenses very seriously. If you come across any illegal copies of our works, in any form, on the Internet, please provide us with the location address or website name immediately so that we can pursue a remedy.

Please contact us at copyright@packtpub.com with a link to the suspected pirated material.

We appreciate your help in protecting our authors, and our ability to bring you valuable content.

Questions

You can contact us at questions@packtpub.com if you are having a problem with any aspect of the book, and we will do our best to address it.

1
Getting Started with Microsoft Dynamics CRM 2011

This chapter is going to give you a basic understanding of Microsoft Dynamics CRM (MS CRM) 2011. We will cover the following topics in this chapter:

- Introduction to Microsoft CRM 2011
- Deployments options
- Microsoft CRM 2011 clients
- Software and hardware requirements for Microsoft CRM 2011
- Modules in Microsoft CRM 2011

Introduction to Microsoft CRM 2011

Every business need to interact with their customers daily to fulfill their different requirements, whether it is for providing them sales, service support, or to inform them about a new product. A **Customer Relationship Management (CRM)** application plays a key role here. Microsoft CRM 2011 is a product that comes in this category. It is a product from the Microsoft Dynamics family, which is a collection of ERP and CRM applications developed by Microsoft. The Microsoft Dynamics family includes the following products:

- Microsoft Dynamics AX
- Microsoft Dynamics GP
- Microsoft Dynamics NAV
- Microsoft Dynamics SL
- Microsoft CRM 2011

Microsoft Dynamics AX, GP, NAV, and SL come in the ERP category and Microsoft CRM 2011 comes in the CRM category. The **Enterprise Resource Planning (ERP)** product is used to manage critical business processes. It includes different modules which help us to manage our different business requirements like finance and budget planning, project, human resources, IT, and supply chain management.

Microsoft CRM 2011 helps businesses to manage their daily activities related to sales, marketing, and service. It helps a business to retain its existing customers as well as to get new customers. Let's take an example of a bike service center. A service center can use Microsoft CRM 2011 to improve their service efficiency using different Microsoft CRM 2011 features. For example, they can use Microsoft CRM 2011 accounts to store their client information with bike service details. They can also create custom entities if required to store service details, and automate the process of service schedules. E-mail activity can be used to send reminders to clients once their service is due. The bike service center can also use the marketing module in Microsoft CRM 2011 to improve marketing process results, by automating their marketing campaign regarding bike service camps and capturing its response. In the same way, the service module in Microsoft CRM 2011 can be used by the service center to provide customer service support. The beauty of Microsoft CRM 2011 is to provide the customer with an interface that is already familiar to them. Everyone has had some experience of Microsoft software, and the interfaces used are standardized. It also provides **out-of-box (OOB)** integration with Microsoft Word, Microsoft Excel, Microsoft Outlook, and Microsoft SharePoint Server. Its conceptual ribbon provides easy navigation to Microsoft CRM 2011 records and commands, which help end users to easily adopt this product after some basic training.

 The OOB term is used to refer to those features that come with the product and don't require any addition installation.

Microsoft CRM 2011 provides rich BI support. We can quickly create a dashboard to monitor our business performance and share it with other users easily. We can use different OOB reports to monitor our sales process. We can also create custom SSRS reports or FetchXML if required, to fill our complex reporting requirements. Custom SSRS reports can be deployed in Microsoft CRM 2011 on-premise deployment whereas FetchXML reports are supported by online as well as on-premises deployment.

Microsoft CRM 2011 is a highly customizable and extendable product. If you are a developer and have knowledge of .NET and JavaScript, you can easily extend Microsoft CRM's functionality. Microsoft CRM 2011 facilitates server-side-code plugins to implement complex business logic. We can also use Microsoft CRM 2011 as a platform to develop any business-specific application. It provides a set of features that are used by any traditional application, such as inbuilt security, workflow support to automate business processes, rich user interface, or the OOB report wizard to create rich BI reports. It also provides you with different personalization options to customize your workplace.

 You can visit `http://msdn.microsoft.com/en-us/ library/gg309589.aspx` to check the new features in Microsoft CRM 2011.

Deployment options

Microsoft CRM 2011 is a web application that can be deployed using the following three models. In the case of an on-premises model, CRM software is installed locally on a single or multiple servers. This deployment is completely controlled by us. By default, on-premises deployments are available only on an intranet. If we want to make them available in an extranet for our end users, then we need to set up IFD. There are two editions for Microsoft CRM 2011 on-premises.

- Workgroup Server 2011
- CRM Server 2011

In the case of the CRM online model, we have to purchase a subscription for CRM software access, which is hosted on Microsoft Servers. The hosted deployment is similar to CRM online, just in this case CRM Server is hosted by third-party vendors instead of Microsoft, so it will be installed in vendors' servers and they will configure IFD to make it available in the extranet.

 You can download the Microsoft CRM 2011 implementation guide at `http://www.microsoft.com/download/en/details. aspx?id=3621` to check configuration details for IFD.

Difference between Microsoft CRM 2011 deployments

The following table explains the difference between features supported by Microsoft CRM 2011 deployments:

Features supported	On-premise	Online	Hosted
Customization	Yes	Yes (we can only create 200 custom entities and 200 custom workflows)	Yes
Plugin development	Yes	Yes (we can register a sandbox plugin in an online deployment)	Yes
Custom workflow	Yes	No	Yes
Internet lead capture	No	Yes	No
Authentication mode	Claims-based or Active Directory authentication	Claims-based or Active Directory (using federation) authentication	Claims-based or Active Directory authentication
Custom JavaScript	Yes	Yes	Yes
Custom reports	Yes (we can use both custom SSRS and FetchXML reports)	Yes (Only FetchXML)	Yes (we can use both custom SSRS and FetchXML reports)

Microsoft CRM 2011 clients

You can access Microsoft CRM 2011 using multiple clients.

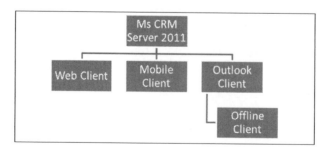

Let's look at each one of them in detail.

Web client

At the time of writing, Microsoft CRM 2011 only supports IE 6 (you need to install SP1 in the case of IE 6.0), IE 7, IE 8, and IE 9. But when this book will be available in the market, I assume the Microsoft CRM 2011 Q4 update will be released. The Microsoft CRM 2011 Q4 2012 update includes multi-browser support for Mozilla Firefox Version 6+, Apple Safari Version 5.1.1+, and Google Chrome Version 13+.

 Note that you can visit `http://crm.dynamics.com/en-us/roadmap` for more details on the Q4 2012 service update.

You can use the following URLs to connect to a CRM environment depending on the deployment type:

- **On-premises:** `http://CRMServerName:port/OrganizationName/`
- **CRM online:** `https://OrganizationName.crm.dynamics.com/`
- **IFD:** `https://OrganizationName.Domain:port`

The following screenshot is an example of accessing Microsoft CRM 2011 on-premise using web client:

 Note that the IFD URL could differ based on organization-specific configuration.

Mobile client

If you have an on-premises installation and you have configured IFD, then you can access your Microsoft CRM 2011 environment from a mobile client. Very soon we are going to get a Microsoft CRM 2011 service update called **CRM Anywhere**, which will allow us to access Microsoft CRM 2011 from most of the latest mobile devices and smartphones. You can also access your CRM online from a mobile client. You need to do a little configuration to access your entity in a mobile client. Go to **Settings | Customization** and select the **Customize the System** option. This will open a default solution for you. Navigate to **Components | Entities** and select the entity that you want to see in your mobile device. Microsoft CRM 2011 has an OOB mobile form that will be displayed when you try to access that entity in your mobile device.

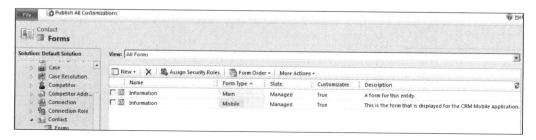

You can click on the form to open it and add the entity fields that you want to see on the mobile form, such as the following:

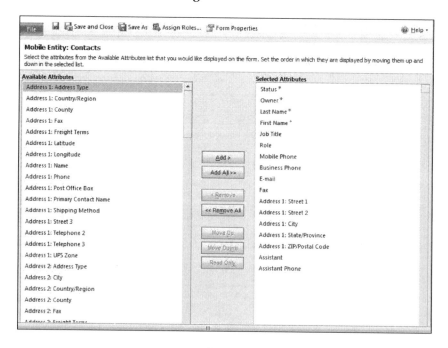

The account, contact, lead, opportunity, and case entities are by default configured for mobile access.

Save and close your changes and publish all the entities. Now you will see the previous entity when you access Microsoft CRM 2011 through your mobile device.

 You need to append /m after your CRM URL while accessing CRM from the mobile client.

Outlook client

You can access your Microsoft CRM 2011 through Microsoft Outlook. While installing Microsoft Outlook for CRM, we can customize installation options to include offline capability or it will install offline capability when you click on the **Go Offline** button on the ribbon toolbar.

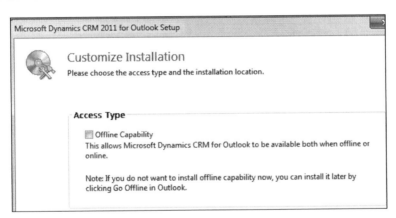

Microsoft CRM for Outlook is used when you are connected to your CRM server all the time. Offline client is designed for those sales executives who work from different locations and are disconnected from the CRM server. They can still use CRM in offline mode in the same way they worked when they were connected. The data entered will be stored locally during this time and their changes will be synchronized when they connect to the CRM server again.

 The workflows and asynchronous plugins are not supported for offline mode.

Software and hardware requirements

The software and hardware requirements can vary based on what type of deployment we are going to use and the number of Microsoft CRM 2011 users. Microsoft CRM 2011 can be installed on Windows 2008 x64 servers.

 Note that Microsoft CRM 2011 only supports 64-bits environment.

Hardware requirements

Component	*Minimum	*Recommended
Processor	x64 architecture or compatible dual-core with 1.5 GHz processor	Quad-core x64 architecture with 2 GHz CPU or higher
Memory	2 GB RAM	8 GB RAM or more
Hard disk	10 GB of available hard disk space	40 GB or more of available hard disk space

Software requirements

Component	Editions
Windows Server	• Windows Server 2008 servers (x64 versions) SP2 or a later version • Windows Web Server 2008 (x64 versions) SP2 or a later version • Windows Small Business Servers 2008 x64 or a later version
SQL Server	Microsoft SQL Server 2008 servers (x64 version) SP1 or a later version
SQL Server Reporting Services	Microsoft SQL Server 2008 Servers (x64 version) SP1 or a later version

Component	Editions
IIS	7.0 or a later version
SharePoint Document Management	• Microsoft SharePoint 2010 (all editions) • Microsoft Office SharePoint Server (MOSS) 2007

> Note that Microsoft SharePoint is required only if you want to use the document management functionality in Microsoft CRM 2011.
>
> You can refer to the Microsoft CRM 2011 implementation guide for details on software and hardware requirements. You can download the Microsoft CRM 2011 implementation guide from `http://www.microsoft.com/en-us/download/details.aspx?id=3621`.

Modules

Microsoft CRM 2011 OOB provides the following three modules:

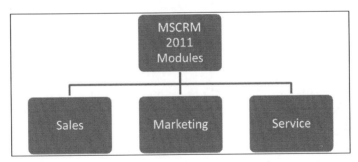

But you can create your custom modules based on your business requirements easily and can use OOB or custom entities in your modules.

Sales module

Sales modules help companies to handle their sales cycle. In Microsoft CRM 2011, the sales cycle starts with a lead. The lead represents a potential customer, which contains basic information about the potential customer. It could be an organization or an individual. Once the lead is generated, it is assigned to a sales person or a team. A sales person will start communicating with the lead to fetch some more information and will update the lead status based on customer interest. Once the lead is qualified, it is converted to the following records type:

- Account
- Contact
- Opportunity

 Note that in Microsoft CRM 2011, both the account and contact entities can represent customers. In a typical scenario, an account represents an organization and a contact represents a person in that organization.

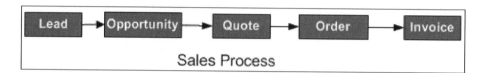

Sales Process

An opportunity represents qualified potential sales. While converting a lead into an opportunity we have to set a potential customer, but if we have selected the **Account** checkbox then CRM will create the account with the **Company name** field in the **Lead** created and will set it as a potential customer of the opportunity. Similarly, if we select **Contact** and **Opportunity** then CRM will set **Contact** as a potential customer in the opportunity.

 If we have selected the **Account**, **Contact**, and **Opportunity** checkboxes, CRM will create an account with the company name in the **Lead** created and will set this account as a parent customer in Contact and potential customer in Opportunity.

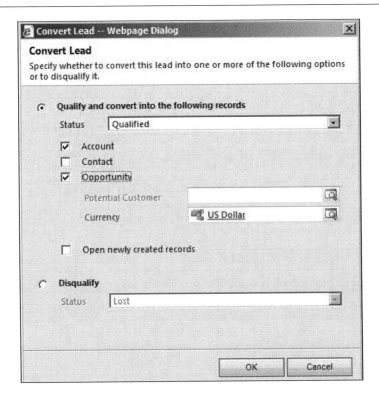

Once an opportunity is created, we can attach a quote to the opportunity to inform the customer about the product and price information. If the customer agrees on the sent quote, we can activate the quote and create an order using **Create Order** ribbon button on the quote form. Once the order is fulfilled, an invoice will be generated using the **Create Invoice** ribbon button on the order form. Once a customer is billed, we can close the opportunity.

Marketing module

Marketing modules deal with all the marketing related activities such as creating a marketing list, creating and sending campaign literature, and capturing its response. In Microsoft CRM 2011, you can create two types of marketing lists:

- Static
- Dynamic

In the case of a static list, we have to add/remove list members manually, but in case of a dynamic list, we can specify our query and based on the query criteria list, members will be added or removed automatically by Microsoft CRM 2011. While creating the list we can select its type to create a static or dynamic list. Let's say we want to create a dynamic marketing list. Select the **dynamic radio** button from the **type** selection and hit the **Save** button. Once the marketing list is saved we can add a query to the dynamic list using the **Manage Members** ribbon button.

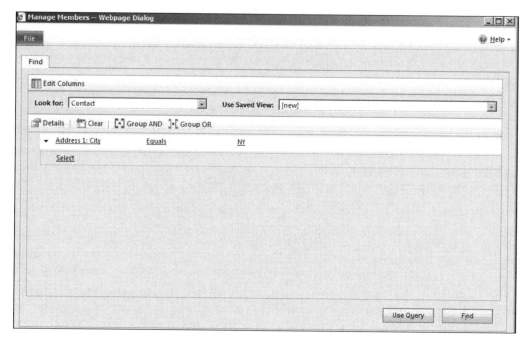

As soon as we will hit the **Use Query** button it will fetch contacts based on the specified query and will add those contacts into our marketing list. Once we have a marketing list ready, we can start creating a new campaign. We can create two types of campaigns in Microsoft CRM 2011:

- Campaign
- Quick campaign

The quick campaign is used to create a single activity campaign, while the campaign can be used to create multiple campaign activities. Creating a campaign includes tasks such as creating **Planning Activities**, **Campaign Activates**, and **Campaign Response** to capture campaign activity responses.

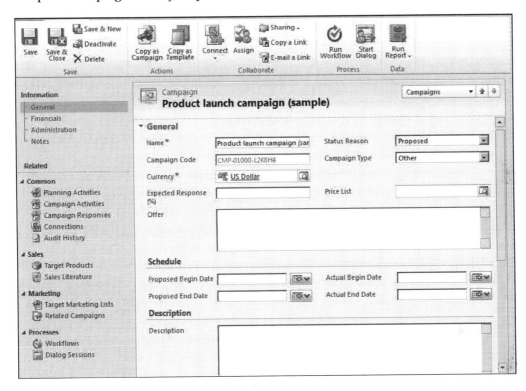

Service module

The service module is used to provide service support to our customer. The service processes start with creating a case in Microsoft CRM 2011. A case contains information about customer services or support requests. A case can be created by a customer service executive or we can automate the process of creating a case in Microsoft CRM 2011 using a queue. We can process a case under a different category by selecting **Subject** from subject lookup in case form.

The Subject is used to classify the case's category in Microsoft CRM 2011. We can create a subject from the **Business Management** section under the **Settings** area in Microsoft CRM 2011.

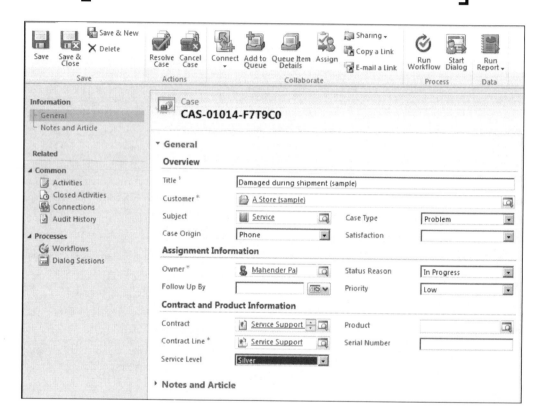

A case can also include contract information. Once the case is created in Microsoft CRM 2011, it is assigned to a customer support executive. The resolution process of a case can include various activities based on the complexity of the case. Sometimes it can be solved by just looking at the Knowledge Base article. Once a case is resolved, the customer support executive can close the case by using the **Resolve Case** ribbon button on the case form. While closing the case, the customer support executive needs to enter information such as resolution type, resolution, and time spent on the resolution process.

The Knowledge Base is basically a collection of articles that contain information about common problem resolutions, best practices, and other technical and functional details.

Summary

Microsoft CRM 2011 helps businesses to retain existing customers as well as get new customers. We have three deployment options, namely on-premises, online, and hosted. The OOB MS CRM 2011 provides three modules, but we can customize Microsoft CRM 2011 to add additional modules based on our business specific requirements. We can access Microsoft CRM 2011 using clients such as browser (web client), Microsoft Outlook, and mobile devices.

2
Customizing Microsoft Dynamics CRM 2011

In this chapter, we are going to use Microsoft Dynamics CRM 2011 to create a sample application called **Project Training Enrollment System (PTES)**. We will explore the different possibilities to customize the Microsoft CRM 2011 application to fit in with our business-specific needs. We will perform requirement analysis for PTES and find out what the different components are that can use OOB and what components we need to customize.

In this chapter we are going to discuss the following topics:

- Project Training Enrolment System
- Requirement analysis for PTES
- Project Training Enrolment System design
- Customization concepts in Microsoft CRM 2011
- Data model for PTES
- System configuration
- Setting up e-mail integration
- Customizing Microsoft CRM 2011 for PTES
- Creating a marketing list
- Using campaign activity in Microsoft CRM 2011
- Capturing the campaign response

Project Training Enrolment System

The project training enrolment system was designed for **Northern Society for Computer Education** (**NSCE**), which is a leading computer education and professional training institute. It provides quality computer education at an affordable fee. The NSCE is going to start a new Project Training Program for its final year students of MCA/BE/MSc (Computers). They are planning to do marketing for their new course, so they need a campaign management system that will help plan an effective marketing campaign and also help them capture the campaign response. Presently they are using a traditional filesystem to store students' data. They are looking for the following features in PTES:

- They should be able to capture institute information within their subbranches
- They should be able to capture student data
- They should be able to automate their campaign process for their new program
- They should be able to capture their campaign response to properly manage the program in the near future
- They should be able to migrate their existing data into a new system
- They should be able to send an e-mail from the new system

Requirement analysis for PTES

NSCE has a key requirement where they want to keep their existing data in the PTES system so that they can use it when there is a future requirement. We need to map Microsoft CRM 2011 OOB entities with their existing data. The NSCE is maintaining two tables, namely Student and Institute. In the Student table, they are storing the students' basic information and address information. In Microsoft CRM 2011, we have a Contact entity that has OOB attributes to store information about a person, so we can use this Contact entity to store student information. We can customize Contact entity fields for our requirement easily. In the Institute table, NSCE is maintaining the institute's basic information and the institute category. In Microsoft CRM 2011, we have an Account entity that is used to store company information and has OOB fields available to store address information and other company details, so we can use this Account entity to track the institute's and its branch offices' information.

Since we mapped an OOB account and Contact entity to store student and institute information, there is no need to create any custom entity. We just need to customize the Account and Contact entities in Microsoft CRM 2011.

Another key requirement from NSCE is that they want to automate their campaign process for the new program that they are going to start. In *Chapter 1, Getting Started with Microsoft Dynamics CRM 2011*, we learned about the marketing module in Microsoft CRM 2011. It is used to deal with all marketing-related activities and has OOB entities, such as marketing lists and campaigns, which can be used to automate the marketing process. So we have decided to use Microsoft CRM's marketing module to create PTES for NSCE. Microsoft CRM 2011 provides default navigation, as shown in the following screenshot, to access its modules; it can easily be customized by modifying the `sitemap.xml` file in Microsoft CRM 2011 based on customer requirements:

We can hide/show the navigation area easily, by modifying the `sitemap.xml` file manually or using the custom tools available for modifying the site map. As NSCE is going to use only the marketing module, we can hide the other modules from Microsoft CRM 2011 navigation.

By going through their requirements, we have identified the following key tasks:

- Changing the Microsoft CRM 2011 application navigation to show only the **My Work, Marketing,** and **Settings** areas on the Microsoft CRM 2011 home page
- Understanding the existing data model and mapoing it with OOB **Account** and **Contact** entities
- Customizing the **Account** entity to capture institute information

- Customizing the **Contact** entity to capture student information
- Removing the **Sales**, **Marketing**, **Service**, and **Process** areas from the left navigation pane of the **Account** and **Contact** entities
- Translations in Microsoft CRM 2011
- Importing the existing data into Microsoft CRM 2011 using the OOB import feature
- Training NSCE to use the marketing module for campaign management

 Note that Microsoft CRM 2011 provides an OOB translation file that is an XML document and can be modified to change the display name of the entity and its attributes.

Project Training Enrolment System Design

We have created the following design for our Project Training Enrollment System. We have mapped the **Institute** and **Branch Office** objects with the Account entity, and mapped the student object with the Contact entity to track student information. We will be using a marketing list to maintain a list of existing students that will be used to distribute **Campaign Activity**.

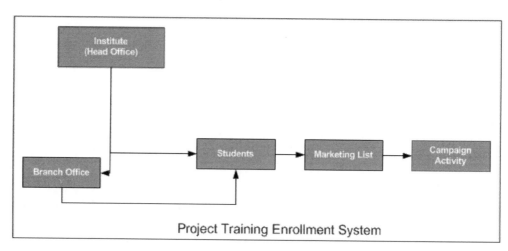

Project Training Enrollment System

Customization concepts in Microsoft CRM 2011

Microsoft Dynamics CRM 2011 provides a very rich application framework that can be easily customized based on our business-specific requirements. By customizing Microsoft CRM 2011, we can change some of its core functionality and add some new functionality to its existing features. Microsoft CRM 2011 can be customized into different levels; it could be a simple UI customization without writing a single line of code or customization that is done by writing some JavaScript code. Most of the Microsoft CRM components can be customized from CRM UI itself.

Data model for PTES

A data model is the most important part of any application. Microsoft CRM 2011 has a different data type available that can be used to map different types of data based on business requirements. Microsoft CRM 2011 has the following data types that can be used to create different types of attributes for the Microsoft CRM 2011 entity:

Data type	Description
Single line of text	This is used to store the string value. We have different options to set its format.
Multiple lines of text	This is used to store the multiple line string; the maximum allowed character is 1048576.
Option set	This is a drop-down list of predefined values; we can create an option set with its own options or create an option set from the global option set.
Two options	This is used to store the Boolean values true/false; we can customize the option label.
Whole number	This is used to store the integer value, which can range from -2147483648 to 214483647.
Floating point number	This is used for double values ranging from -100000000000 to 100000000000; the maximum number of allowed decimal places is five.
Decimal number	This is used to store decimal values ranging from -100000000000 to 100000000000; 10 decimal places are allowed.
Currency	This is used to store the amount of money; when we add the currency field, another base field is added automatically.
Date and time	This is used to store the date and time value.
Lookup	This is used to create an entity relationship.

We have identified the data model that can be used to capture institute and student information in PTES. Refer *Appendix A, Data Model*, for more information.

Customizing existing fields

Based on the identified data model, most of the attributes from the Account and Contact entities can be used as they are without any customization, but we need to customize some of the existing fields. Perform the following steps to modify the existing fields:

1. Navigate to **Setting | Customization | Customize the System** from the Microsoft CRM 2011 home page. Microsoft CRM 2011 will open the default solution for us.

2. Expand **Entities**, select the entity to be modified, and select **Fields**.

3. Double-click on the field that we want to modify to open the field property window. We are going to modify the **Category** field to add our custom values.

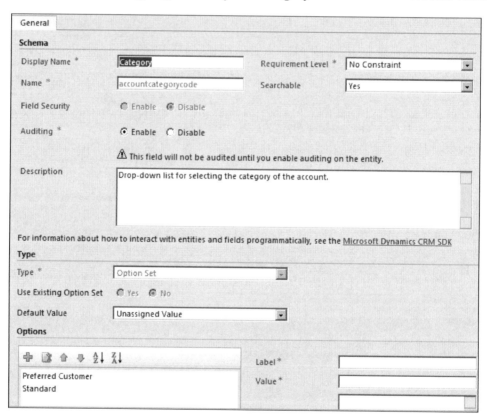

4. Select the first option from **Options** and change **Label** to Head Office.

5. Select the second option from **Options** and change **Label** to Branch Office.

6. Click on **Save and Close**.

7. Select your entity and click on **Publish** from the solution ribbon toolbar.

System configuration

We are using the Microsoft CRM 2011 on-premise deployment for our PTES application. We have installed the Microsoft CRM 2011 application on a single server. One key requirement for PTES is to capture the campaign responses in Microsoft CRM to track the effectiveness of the campaign. Microsoft CRM 2011 provides OOB marketing entities that can be used to implement the marketing process. We can use the Campaign Response entity to automate the campaign response creation process in Microsoft CRM. For example, when we create an e-mail campaign activity in our campaign and distribute it, Microsoft CRM 2011 will create individual e-mail activity records based on the marketing list members who have subject information in the related field. If the recipient of the e-mail sends back an e-mail in reply, Microsoft CRM will automatically match the incoming message with the e-mail activity based on the information in the e-mail subject. If Microsoft CRM finds a match, it creates a corresponding campaign response activity. For this, we need to enable e-mail tracking in Microsoft CRM. Perform the following steps to enable e-mail tracking:

1. In the navigation pane, click on **Settings** and then click on **Administration**.

2. Click on **System Settings**.

3. In the **System Settings** dialog box, click on the **E-mail** tab.

4. Set the tracking options for e-mails between CRM users.

5. Click on the **Marketing** tab and then verify that **Create campaign response for incoming e-mail** is set to **Yes**.

6. Click on **OK** to save your changes and close the **System Settings** dialog box.

Setting up e-mail integration

In order to send an e-mail from Microsoft CRM 2011, we need to set up e-mail integration. Mainly, we have the following two options for e-mail integration:

- Using an e-mail router
- Using CRM for the Microsoft Outlook client

Both options have their own pros and cons. Please refer to `http://blogs.msdn.com/b/crm/archive/2008/02/07/crm-4-0-e-mail-integration-overview.aspx` for more details about e-mail integration.

We have an e-mail router installed in our development server, so we are going to use this e-mail router. Before setting up the e-mail router, we need to configure mail access for every CRM user. We need to perform the following steps to set e-mail access configuration to use the e-mail router:

1. Navigate to the **System Configuration** section from the Microsoft CRM home page.

2. Select **Administration | Users**.

3. Open the user record and set **E-mail Router** in both the incoming and outgoing settings, as shown in the following screenshot:

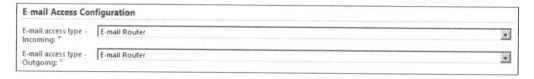

Configuring e-mail router for PTES

We need to set up e-mail integration so that we can distribute the e-mail activity created for the campaign. We can send an e-mail from Microsoft CRM using the following two options:

*   Microsoft Outlook
*   E-mail router

We are going to use an e-mail router for the integration of our e-mail. First we need to download the e-mail router from `http://www.microsoft.com/download/en/details.aspx?id=27818`. After the e-mail router is installed, we need to configure the e-mail router. We will be performing the steps explained in the next section to configure the e-mail router.

Configuration profiles

First we need to configure at least one profile, depending on our requirement regarding e-mail integration. For example, if we are only going to send e-mails from Microsoft CRM, then we will configure an outgoing profile, and if we are only going to receive e-mails in Microsoft CRM, we will just configure an incoming profile.

Perform the following steps to configure the profiles:

1. Select the **Configuration Profiles** tab and click on **New** to create a new profile.

2. We need to set up the following information to configure an incoming or outgoing profile:

    1. **Profile Name**: Enter the name of the profile here.

    2. **E-mail Server Type**: Here we set up the e-mail server types for the incoming and outgoing profiles.

       For the incoming profile, the e-mail router supports the Exchange Server 2003/2007/2010/Online exchange or POP3 e-mail systems.

       For the outgoing profile, the e-mail router supports only the Exchange Online or SMTP e-mail system.

    3. **Authentication Type**: We have three options to set the authentication type.

       The first option is **Windows Authentication**. This authentication type is available if we are using Microsoft Exchange Server for incoming e-mail.

       The second option is **NTLM**. This option is available only if we are using POP3 for the incoming profile.

       The third option is **Clear Text**. This option is available if we are using POP3 or the Online Exchange server.

    4. **Location**: We enter the name of the e-mail server.

5. **Access Type**: Depending on the other configuration profile options, we need to set up the access type, where we can provide the **User name** and **Password** that the e-mail router will use to access each mailbox.

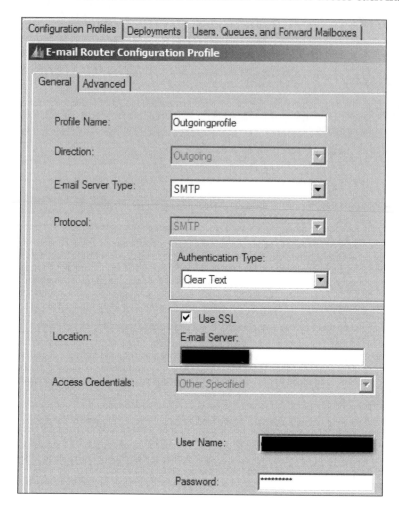

Deployments

In Deployments, we need to mention our organization name along with the incoming and outgoing profiles that we created in the previous section:

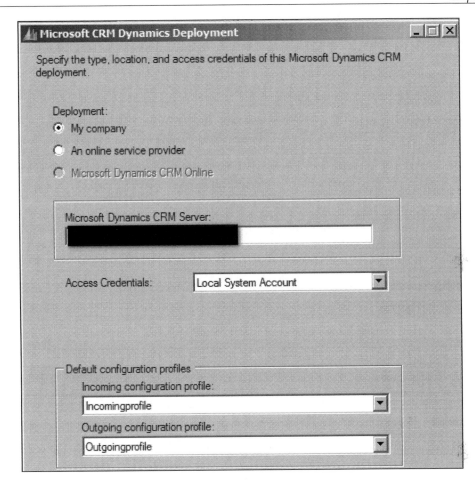

Configuring users, queues, and the forward mailbox

Once we have configured our profile and deployed it, we need to set up users and queues. Perform the following steps to configure the users and queues:

1. Navigate to the **Users, Queues, and Forward Mailboxes** tab.

2. Select our deployment from the deployment drop-down menu.

3. Click on **Load Data** to load the list of users and queues that were configured to use the e-mail router.

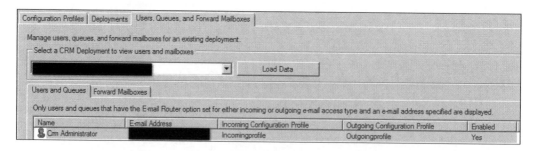

4. Once the user is configured, we can click on the **Test Access** button to test the connection with the e-mail servers, and click on **Publish** to publish the settings for the e-mail router.

 You can download the e-mail router configuration guide from http://www.microsoft.com/download/en/ details.aspx?id=21445.

Customizing Microsoft CRM 2011 for PTES

Now we have e-mail integration configured, let's start customizing MS CRM 2011 for our PTES. We are using the Microsoft CRM 2011 on-premise deployment for this application. In the next section, we will customize application navigation of Microsoft CRM 2011.

Changing Microsoft CRM 2011 application navigation

Application navigation can easily be controlled by customizing the site map in Microsoft CRM. We have two options to modify the site map: either we can manually export our solution and customize the site map, or we can use any custom site map editor tool. We are going to use SiteMap Editor for Microsoft CRM 2011 written by the Microsoft Dynamics CRM 2011 MVP, Tanguy Touzard. You can download SiteMap Editor from http://sitemapeditor.codeplex.com/.

Once we have downloaded this tool, we need to open `SiteMapEditor.exe` to create a connection to our CRM organization. Select the **Create new connection** option from the drop-down menu available in the bottom left-hand corner of the editor.

After connecting with our organization, we need to click on the **Load SiteMap** button in the SiteMap editor window to load the default site map. Once the default site map is loaded, we can remove the unwanted navigation sections from the site map.

 We can also control site map navigation based on the security role. Please refer to `rc.crm.dynamics.com/rc/regcont/en_us/ live/articles/controlAccessToRC.aspx` for more details.

To rename the left navigation sections, we need to select them and write a new label in the **Title** field, and hit the **Save** button. Once our modification is over, we can click on the **Update SiteMap** button to update the site map in Microsoft CRM. After modifying the site map, we need to refresh the Microsoft CRM home page to see the changes in the left navigation area.

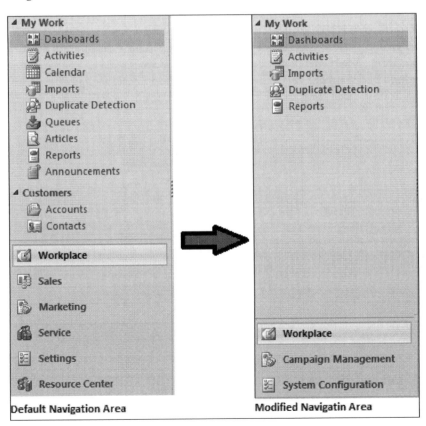

Note that you can refer to the SiteMap Editor documentation at `http://sitemapeditor.codeplex.com/documentation`.

Solution

There are many new enhancement features in Microsoft CRM 2011, and **Solution** is one of them. Solution is a collection of various components that can be created or customized. Using Solution, we can distribute our customization, custom assembly, and other components under a single unit. It is always recommended to include only those components in Solution that you have customized or created. While creating Solution, we need to make sure that we are including all the required dependencies; otherwise, we can face issues when we try to import this Solution into another environment. There are two types of Solution:

- Managed
- Unmanaged

Every Microsoft CRM 2011 implementation contains one default, Unmanaged Solution. This contains all the components that were created during the installation of the Microsoft CRM application. When we create a new Solution, it is created in an unmanaged state. But when a Solution is complete and ready to be distributed, it can be exported as a Managed Solution. A Solution can contain the **Components** shown in the following screenshot:

If we need to import our Solution in a production environment, it is recommended to export it as a Managed Solution. If an Unmanaged Solution is imported to another environment, it can be modified easily. However, in Solution we can set up properties for the component so it won't allow the user to modify it if it is exported as a Managed Solution.

Managed Solutions can be uninstalled easily from the Microsoft CRM 2011 environment, but Unmanaged Solutions do not provide any facility to uninstall them. We need to manually delete its component if we need to uninstall it. While creating a Solution, we need to specify its publisher. The publisher represents an owner of the Solution.

 Note that it's recommended to have the same Rollup installed in the source and target systems before exporting and importing the Solution.

Creating Solution for PTES

We can create Solution in Microsoft CRM 2011 using the following steps:

1. Select **System Configuration** (we have changed the **Setting** label to **System Configuration** now) from the Microsoft CRM home page's screen.

2. Select **Solution** in the **Customization** area.

3. Select **New** from the Solution toolbar and enter the following information:

Display Name	Project Training Enrollment System
Name	This will be created automatically based on Display Name
Publisher	Select the default publisher for NSCE from the publisher lookup
Version	1.0

Once the Solution is created, we can add the required component to it. We need to add the Account, Contact, and Marketing List entities to our Solution.

Adding components in Solution

Perform the following steps to add the Account and Contact entities to our Solution:

1. Select **Entities** from the left navigation pane in our Solution.

2. Click on the **Add Existing** button in Solution; this will open a dialog box from which you can select the entities.

3. Select **Account, Contact,** and **Marketing list,** and click on **OK** to add these entities to our Solution.

Once we have added the Account and Contact entities to our Solution, we can rename the entities and their attributes. Navigate to the **Account** entity from **Component | Entities.**

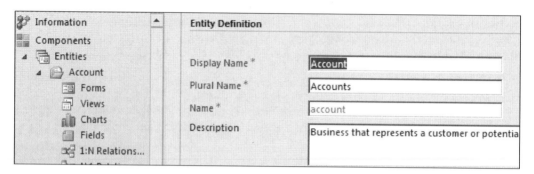

Change the following information in the **Entity Definition** section and click on the **Save** button from the **Solution** toolbar:

- **Display Name**: **Institute**
- **Plural Name**: **Institutes**

After saving, the **Account** entity name should be changed to **Institute,** and it should look like the following screenshot:

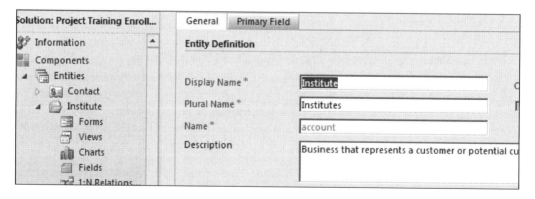

Once Account is renamed to **Institute,** we need to customize all the views to change their name properties. Navigate to **Views** and open the views one by one to change the view name. We need to perform the following steps to rename the views:

1. Select the **Active** contact and select **Edit** from the **More Actions** drop-down menu. This will open the **Active** contact view in edit mode.

2. Select **View Properties** from the **common task** section.

3. Change the name of the view.

4. Follow the previous steps to changes all the view names.

Now we need to change the name of the **Fields** property. Navigate to **Fields** from the **Institute** entity and change **Display Name** of the fields one by one based on the data model for Institute entity. For the data model, refer *Appendix A, Data model*. After customizing the fields, we need to modify the **Institute** form to place only those fields that are required to capture institute information.

Navigate to **Form** under the **Institute** entity and open the **Main** form to remove unwanted fields and sections. We have to include all the fields in the data model table in the **Institute** form.

Remove sales, marketing, and service area

We have faced this requirement in many Microsoft CRM 4.0 implementations, where the user has asked to remove the unwanted left navigation pane from Microsoft CRM entity forms. In Microsoft CRM 4.0, there were two options to remove unwanted left navigation pane items:

1. By setting **Do Not Display** in the relationship tab.

2. By using JavaScript.

In Microsoft CRM 2011, apart from the preceding two options, we have one other option to remove them directly. Perform the following steps to remove the left-hand navigation area from the **Institute** form:

1. Double-click on the left navigation pane to highlight it.

2. Select the subitems under **Sales** and click on the **Remove** button from the ribbon toolbar.

3. Remove all the subitems from the **Sales**, **Marketing**, **Service**, and **Processes** sections one by one.

4. Click on **Save**.

5. Click on **Publish** to publish the Institute form.

After making all these changes, the Institute form should like the following screenshot:

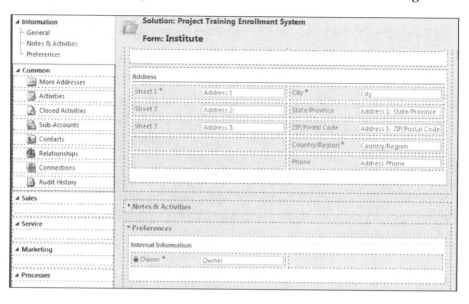

We need to follow all these steps to rename the Contact entity and its attribute, and we need to delete the left navigation pane items from the Contact form. We can remove the unwanted left navigation pane items one by one.

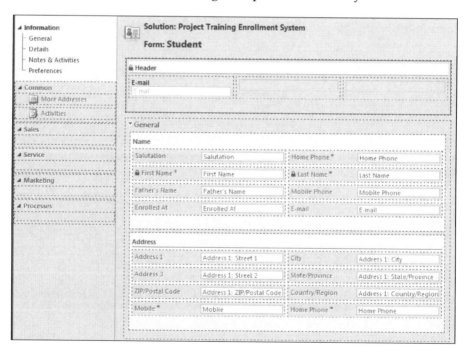

Changing translations in Microsoft CRM 2011

After changing the entities, fields, and view properties, we need to change various labels for the Account and Contact entities. We can do this by exporting the translation file from Microsoft CRM 2011. Perform the following steps to change the translations in Microsoft CRM 2011:

1. Click on the **Export Translations** button from the Solution toolbar. This will open the file download dialog box.

2. Save the ZIP folder to some location and extract the content from this folder.

3. Open the `CrmTranslations.xml` file in excel to edit it.

4. Select the **Display Strings** sheet and select the last column.

5. Open the **Find and Replace** dialog box and replace Account with Institute and Contact with Student.

6. Select the **Localized Labels** sheet, select the last column, and repeat the previous step.

7. Save and close the file; compress that folder again and import it in Microsoft CRM 2011.

Importing existing student data into Microsoft CRM 2011

Once the customization part is over, we need to migrate the existing data into Microsoft CRM 2011. Microsoft CRM 2011 Import Wizard now supports the import of multiple file types. We can import `.xml`, `.csv`, `.txt`, and `.zip` files. We cannot import individual files of more than 8 MB. If we need to import more than 8 MB, we can import ZIP files. We cannot import ZIP files bigger than 32MB. First we need export data import templates from Microsoft CRM 2011. Perform the following steps to export the data template for the Institute and Student entities:

1. Navigate to **System Configuration** and select **Data Management**.

2. Click on **Templates for Data Import**.

3. Select **Institute** as the record type and click on **Download**.

4. We also need to download a template for the Student entity using the same method.

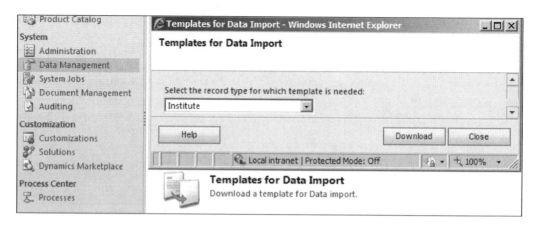

Once we have exported both entities' templates, we need to fill data in the exported template in the required format. We need to open the exported templates in Microsoft Excel. While entering the data, we need to make sure that we are filling the data in the proper format. When we open the template in Microsoft Excel, it will show field details in the tool tip.

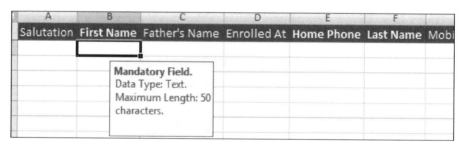

Perform the following steps to import the data to the Student entity:

1. Navigate to **Imports** under the **My Work** area.
2. Click on the **Import Data** button on the application ribbon.

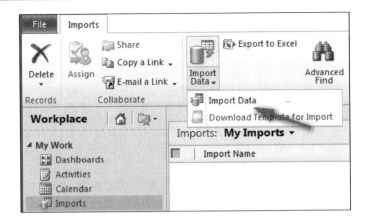

3. Click on **Browse** and select the Student.xml file.

4. Click on **Next**; make sure all the fields are mapped accordingly.

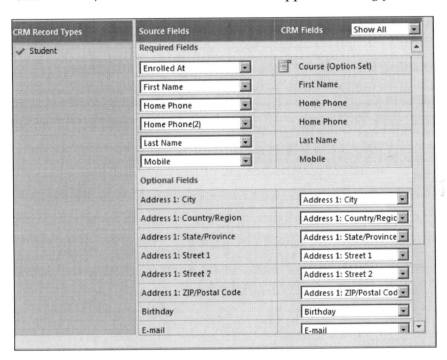

5. Click on **Next** and select **No** from the **Allow Duplicate** section.

6. Click on **Submit** to submit the imported data.

7. Click on **Finish**.

Navigate to **Import** under **My work** and check the **My Import** view to check the status of our import.

 Please refer to http://msdn.microsoft.com/en-us/library/gg328321.aspx for more details on data import in Microsoft CRM 2011.

Creating a marketing list

Now that we have everything in place, it's time to use student data and create a marketing list.

Perform the following steps to create a marketing list:

1. Navigate to the **Marketing** section from the CRM home page.

2. Select **Marketing List** from the left navigation pane and select **New** to create a new marketing list.

3. Enter the following basic information:
   - **Name**: Project Trainee List
   - **Member Type**: Student
   - **Type**: Static
   - **Purpose**: Campaign

4. Click on the **Manage Members** button from the ribbon toolbar.

5. Select the **Use Advance Find to add members** option from the **Manage Members** dialog box, and click on **OK**.

6. Add a condition to include the students who have enrolled for Btech, MCA, and MSc Computers, as shown in the following screenshot, and click on **Find**:

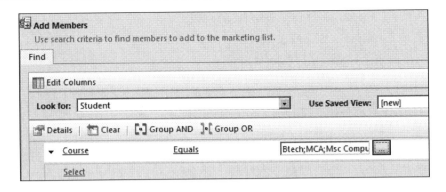

7. Select all the records from the result set and click on the **Add to Marketing List** button.

8. Click on **Save and Close**.

Using campaign activity in Microsoft CRM 2011

After creating a marketing list, we need to plan our campaign. Campaign is a container for all the information and activities used to create our campaign. Campaign activities are used as a communication channel to pass information to our client. While creating a campaign, there are mainly two activities involved:

- Planning activities
- Creating campaign activities

Campaign planning activities are used to track all the activities that we are going to create for our campaign. This helps us organize the activity sequence that we are going to use in our campaign. Creating campaign activities is similar to planning activities, but it includes more detailed information about the pricing. Perform the following steps to create the campaign:

1. Navigate to **Campaign** under the **Marketing** area in the Microsoft CRM home page.

2. Select **New** to create the campaign, and enter the following basic details and hit the **Save** button:
   - **Name: Project Training Enrolment Programme**
   - **Campaign Code: NSCE01**

       ◦   **Campaign Type: Advertisement**

       ◦   **Budget Allocated: 12000**

       ◦   **Miscellaneous Costs: 2000**

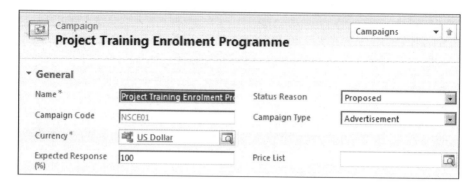

3. In the left navigation pane in the **Marketing** section, click on **Target Marketing Lists**.

4. Click on **Add Existing Marketing List**.

5. Select **Project Trainee List** and click on **OK**.

Planning activities for our campaign

Now that we have created a campaign record, it's time to plan our campaign activities. At this moment, we are just going to create one e-mail activity. Perform the following steps to create a planning activity:

1. Navigate to **Planning Activities**.

2. On the **List Tools Activities** tab in the **Records** group, click on **Add New Activity**.

3. Select **E-mail activity** and enter the following information:

       ◦   **Subject**: Enter details of the e-mail template

       ◦   **Description**: Design an appropriate e-mail message for sending in campaign activity

4. Click on **Save and Close**.

Adding campaign activity

Perform the following steps to add the campaign activity:

1. Navigate to **Campaign Activities** under the **Common** section in the left navigation pane.

2. Click on the **Add New Campaign Activity** button from the ribbon toolbar under the **Campaign Activities** tab.

3. Fill in the following information:
   - **Channel**: E-mail
   - **Subject**: Enter information regarding Professional Project Training Course
   - **Type**: Research

4. Click on **Save** to save the campaign activity.

Distributing the campaign activity

We have created a campaign and campaign activity, and it's time to distribute our campaign activity to the marketing list members. Perform the following steps to distribute the campaign activity:

1. Click on the **Distribute Campaign Activity** button on the ribbon from the **Campaign Activity** tab.

2. Fill the **Subject** field and description in the e-mail, as shown in the following screenshot:

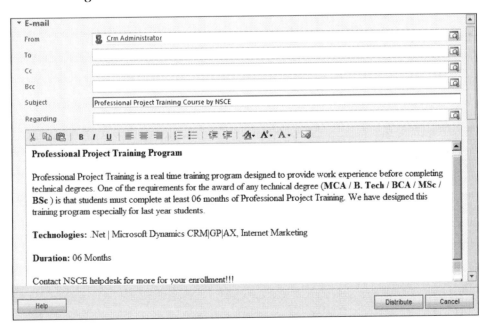

3. Click on the **Distribute** button.

4. Select the **I will own the new E-mail Messages** radio button from the confirmation dialog box.

Capturing the campaign response

After distributing our campaign activities, our next task is to track the campaign response. Microsoft CRM 2011 provides different methods to capture a campaign response:

- Creating the campaign response manually
- Converting an existing campaign activity to a campaign response
- Generating the campaign response automatically
- Importing campaign response data in Microsoft CRM

We have configured Microsoft CRM 2011 to automatically generate a campaign response for us. So when a customer replies to our campaign e-mail, Microsoft CRM 2011 will create a corresponding campaign response activity based on the subject of our campaign activity. Perform the following steps to check the campaign response:

1. Navigate to the **Campaign Management** section from the Microsoft CRM home page, and select **Campaign**.

2. Select the **Project Training Enrolment Programme** campaign record and double-click to open it.

3. Navigate to **Campaign Responses** under the **Common** section from the left navigation pane.

We will get a campaign, as shown in the following screenshot:

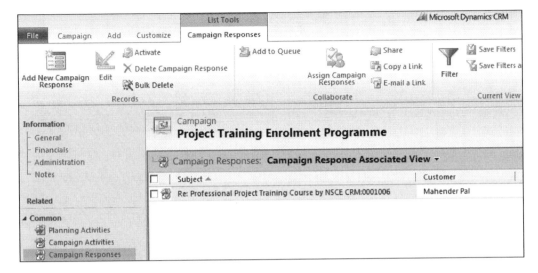

Summary

In this chapter, we used the Microsoft CRM 2011 marketing module to create a Project Training Enrolment System. We learned how we can customize the Microsoft CRM 2011 application interface to fulfill our business specific needs. We learned how to use SiteMap Editor to customize site map navigation in Microsoft CRM 2011. We created a marketing list, and learned how to use this marketing list in campaign activity and to capture a campaign response.

In the next chapter, we will see how we can use Microsoft CRM 2011 to automate an employee recruitment process.

3
Using Processes in Microsoft Dynamics CRM 2011

In this chapter, we are going to use Microsoft Dynamics CRM 2011 as a platform to develop our **Employee Recruitment Management System (ERMS)**. We will learn the basics of ERMS, about processes in Microsoft CRM 2011, and how we can use them to automate business processes at different levels.

In this chapter we are going to discuss the following topics:

- Employee Recruitment Management System
- Employee Recruitment Management System design
- Setting a security model for Employee Recruitment Management System
- Setting field-level security
- Data model for Employee Recruitment Management System
- Customizing entities for Employee Recruitment Management System
- Setting a security model for ERMS
- Setting field-level security in Microsoft CRM 2011
- Processes in Microsoft CRM 2011
- Importing data in Microsoft CRM 2011
- Testing Employee Recruitment Management System

Employee Recruitment Management System basics

Hiring the right candidate is a challenge for the recruitment team of any company. The process of hiring candidates can differ from company to company. Different sources such as job sites, networking, and consulting firms can be used to get the right candidate, but most companies prefer to hire a candidate from their own employee network. Before starting the hiring process, a recruiter should have a proper understanding of the candidate profile that fits the company's requirements.

Normally, this process starts by screening candidate resumes fetched from different sources. Once they have resumes of appropriate candidates, the recruitment team starts working on resumes one by one. Recruiters talk to potential candidates and enquire about their skills and test their interpersonal skills. Recruiters play an important role in the hiring process; they prepare candidates for interview and provide interview feedback.

Employee Recruitment Management System design

In the employee recruitment applications, we will be using the key objects shown in the following figure to capture the required information:

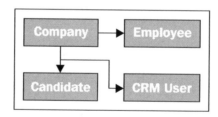

The blocks perform the following tasks:

- **Company**: This block stores the company details
- **Candidate**: This block stores information about the candidate profile
- **Employee**: This block stores employee data
- **CRM User**: This block stores Microsoft CRM user information

As we are going to use Microsoft CRM 2011 as a platform to build our application, let's map these key blocks with Microsoft CRM 2011 entities:

- Company: The term "account" in Microsoft CRM represents an organization, so we can map the company object with an account entity and can store company information in the account entity.
- Candidate: The Candidate object will store information about suitable candidates for our company. We will use the candidate entity to store all interview related feedback, other position details, and address information. We are going to map the candidate entity with a lead entity, because it has most of the fields OOB that we need for our candidate entity.
- Employee: In Microsoft CRM 2011 sales process, when lead is qualified, it is converted to an account, a contact, and an opportunity, so we utilize this process for our application. When a candidate is selected, we will convert the candidate to an employee using the OOB process, which will map all the candidate information to the Candidate entity automatically.

 When a lead is converted to an account or contact or opportunity, the lead record is deactivated by Microsoft CRM 2011.

Let's talk about the process flow that we are going to use in our employee recruitment application. Recruiters will start the process of hiring a candidate by importing candidate resumes in Microsoft CRM under the Candidate entity; we will customize our OOB entities to include the required information. Once data is imported in Microsoft CRM, the recruiter will start the screening of candidates one by one. He will schedule Technical, Project Manager, and finally HR rounds. Once the candidate is selected the recruiter will create an offer letter for that candidate, send it to the respective candidate, and convert the Candidate entity to Employee. The following flowchart shows our employee recruitment application process flow:

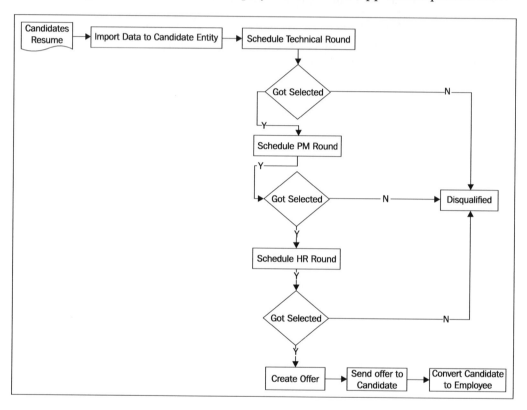

Data model

We have identified the data model for required entities. We need to customize OOB entities based on the data model tables.

Please refer to *Appendix A, Data Model*, for the data model.

Customizing entities for Employee Recruitment Management System

Once we have the data model ready, we need to customize the Microsoft CRM UI and OOB entities. Let's first create our solution called HR Module and add the required entities to that solution.

 Refer to the solution in the *Customizing Microsoft CRM 2011 for PTES* section in *Chapter 2, Customizing Microsoft Dynamics CRM 2011*, to create a solution in Microsoft CRM 2011.

Customizing Microsoft CRM UI

We need to customize the Microsoft CRM site map. We have options to modify the sitemap manually or using the site map editor tool that we used in *Chapter 2, Customizing Microsoft Dynamics CRM 2011*. We need to customize the site map based on the following table; follow *Chapter 2, Customizing Microsoft Dynamics CRM 2011* to customize the site map:

Sr No	Customization Detail
1	Remove Left Navigation: **Marketing, Service, Resource Center**
2	Rename Left Navigation: Sales to **HR Module**, Setting to **Configuration**
3	Remove Left Navigation items under **My Work: Queues, Articles, Announcements**
4	Remove all Left Navigation items under **HR Module** left navigation: except **Lead, Accounts, and Contacts**

After customizing the site map, Microsoft CRM UI should look like the following screenshot:

 It is recommended that you comment unwanted navigation areas out of the site map instead of removing them.

Customizing OOB entities

After we have customized Microsoft CRM UI, we need to rename the entity and entity views. We also need to perform the following actions:

- Renaming OOB entities: We need to rename the lead, account, and contact entities to candidate, company, and employee. Open the entities in edit mode and rename them as described in *Chapter 2, Customizing Microsoft Dynamics CRM 2011.*

- Changing Translation labels: After renaming the OOB entities, we need to change the translation labels in Microsoft CRM. We need to convert Lead to Candidate and Contact to Employee. Please refer to *Chapter 2, Customizing Microsoft Dynamics CRM 2011*, to change translation labels in Microsoft CRM.

Creating/customizing entity fields:

We need to create and customize entity fields; based on the data model we just saw, let's create candidate entity fields. Use the following steps to create fields:

1. Open our **HRModule** solution.

2. Navigate to **Entities | Candidate | Fields**.

3. Click on **New** to create a new field.

4. Enter the following field properties:

   - **Display Name**: Text that you want to show to the user on the form.

   - **Name**: This will be populated automatically as we tab out from the **Display Name** field.

    The **Display Name** field is used as a label in Microsoft CRM 2011 entity form and views, whereas the **Name** field is used to refer to the field in code.

   - **Requirement Level**: Used to enforce data validation on the form.

   - **Searchable**: If this is true, this field will be available in the **Advance Finds** field list.

   - **Field Security**: Used to enable field-level security. It is a new feature added in Microsoft CRM 2011. Refer to the *Setting field-level security in Microsoft CRM 2011* section for more details.

   - **Auditing**: Used to enable auditing for entity fields. It is also a new feature added in Microsoft CRM 2011. Using auditing, we can track entity and attribute data changes for an organization. You can refer to `http://msdn.microsoft.com/en-us/library/gg309664.aspx` for more details on the auditing feature.

   - **Description**: Used to provide additional information about fields.

   - **Type**: Represents what type of data we are going to store in this field; based on the type selected, we need to set other properties.

    You can't change the data type of a created field, but you can change its properties.

After filling in this information, our entity form should look like the following screenshot:

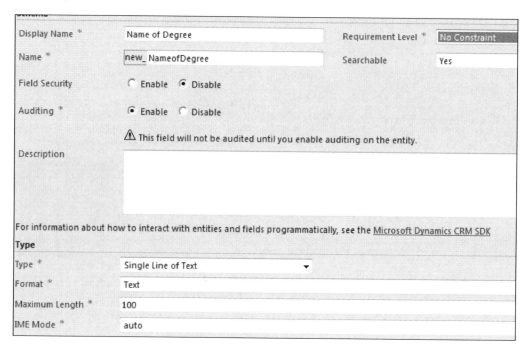

We need to create fields for all entities based on the preceding steps, one by one.

Setting relationship mapping

In Microsoft CRM 2011, we can relate two entities by creating a relationship between them. We can create three types of relationships:

- One-to-many relationship: A one-to-many relationship is created between one primary entity and many related entities. Microsoft CRM 2011 creates a relationship field (lookup field) automatically for each related entity when a one-to-many relationship is created.

 We can create a self-relationship by selecting a primary entity on both sides.

- Many-to-one relationship: A many-to-one relationship is created between many related entities and one primary entity.

- Many-to-many relationship: A many-to-many relationship can be created between many related entities. To create a many-to-many relationship, the user must have Append and Append To privileges in both side entities.

 We can define different relationship behaviors while creating a relationship; you can refer to `http://msdn.microsoft.com/en-us/library/gg309412.aspx` for more details.

After creating a relationship, we can define a mapping to transfer values from parent entity to child entity, but this functionality can only achieved when a child entity record is created from a parent entity using the **Add New** button from the **Associated** view We need to set up relationship mapping so that we can take the candidate field values to the employee entity when the recruiter converts a candidate into an employee. Use the following steps to set the mapping:

1. Navigate to **1:N Relationship** under the **Candidate** entity.
2. Open the **contact_originating_lead** mapping to edit it.
3. Navigate to **Mapping** and click on **New** to add a mapping.
4. Select **new_variablecompensation** from the Source and Target entities and click on **OK**.
5. Follow step 4 to add mapping for the fields shown in the following screenshot:

	Source Name	Source Display Name	Target Name ▼	Target Display Name
	new_variablecompensation	Variable Compensation	new_variablecompensation	Variable Compensation
	new_positionappliedfor	Position Applied For	new_role	Role
	new_nameofdegree	Name of Degree	new_nameofdegree	Name Of Degree
	new_fixed	Fixed	new_fixedsalary	Fixed
	new_degree	Academic Qualification	new_degree	Degree

Form design

Now we need to design forms for our entity, and we need to remove unnecessary fields from entity forms.

Use the following steps to customize entity forms:

1. Open the solution that we created.
2. Navigate to **Entity | Account | Forms**.

3. Open the main form to modify it, as shown in the following screenshot:

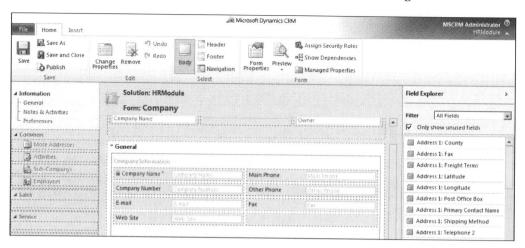

We can remove unwanted fields easily by selecting them one by one and using the **Remove** ribbon button on the entity form. To place the field, we just need to drag-and-drop it from the right-hand side field explorer.

Account form design

Once we have customized the account entity, we need to design the account form shown in the following screenshot:

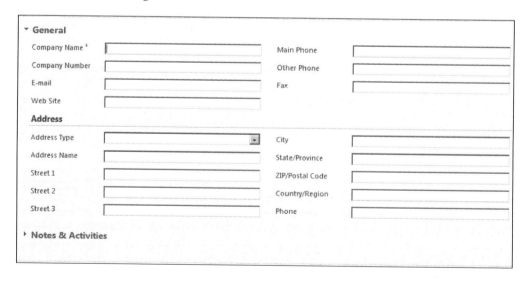

Candidate form design

The candidate form should look like the following screenshot after customization:

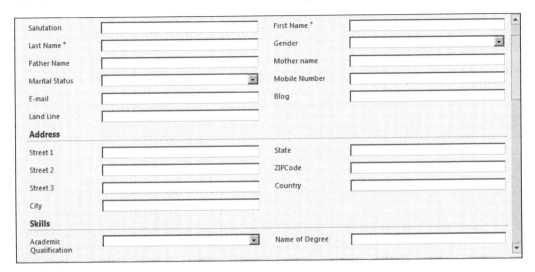

Employee form design

After removing unwanted fields and adding required fields, the employee form should look like the following screenshot:

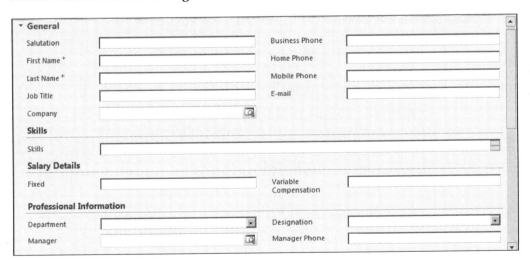

Setting a security model for ERMS

Microsoft CRM provides us the OOB security model that helps us to prevent unauthorized access to our data. We can enforce security in Microsoft CRM using security roles. A security role is a combination of different privileges and access levels.

- **Privileges**: These are actions such as **Create, Write, Delete, Read, Append, Append To, Assign, Share**, and **Reparent** that a Microsoft CRM user can perform on entities. The list of the actions performed is as follows:
    - **Create**: This action is used to create an entity record
    - **Read**: This action is used to read an entity record
    - **Write**: This action is used to modify an entity record
    - **Delete**: This action is used to delete an entity record
    - **Append**: This action is used to relate one entity record to another entity record
    - **Append To**: This action is used to relate other entity records to the current entity record
    - **Share**: This action is used to share an entity record with another user
    - **Reparent**: This action is used to assign a different owner to an entity record

- **Access level**: This defines on which entity record a Microsoft CRM user can perform actions defined by privileges. We have the following actions under access levels:
    - Organization: This action is used to provide access to all records in an organization
    - Parent-child Business Unit: This action is used to provide access to all the records in the user's business unit as well as in all child business units of the user's business unit
    - Business: This action is used to provide access to all records in the user's business unit
    - User: This action allows the user to access records created by him/her, or shared with him/her, or shared with his/her team

We must assign at least one security role to access Microsoft CRM applications. Microsoft CRM provides us with 14 OOB security roles that can be customized based on our requirements. The following diagram is the security-role hierarchy that we have identified for the Employee Management System:

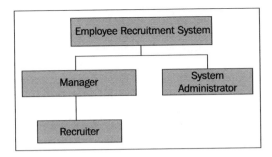

The blocks in the preceding diagram can be explained as follows:

- **HR Manager**: This role will have access to all information for an employee in the ERMS system
- **Recruiter**: This role will not have access to information about offered packages to an employee
- **System Administrator**: This role will have administrative privileges and will be responsible for customizing and maintaining ERMS

We will be customizing the existing security roles for our ERMS. The following table shows the security role mapping that we be will using:

Microsoft CRM Security Role	ERMS Security Role
Sales Manager	Manager
Salesperson	Recruiter
System Administrator	System Administrator

Customizing the existing security role

We need to use the following steps to customize the existing security role:

1. Navigation to **Setting | Administration | Security Roles**.
2. Double-click on the **Sales Manager** role to open it in edit mode.
3. Change **Role Name** to Manager.
4. Click on **Save and then on Close**.
5. Follow the same steps to change the name of the **Sales Person** role to Recruiter.

You can also create a new **Manager Security** role by copying the **Sales Manager** role.

Once we have changed the security role name, we need to configure the **Security Manager** and **Recruiter** roles to remove unnecessary privileges. Follow the ensuing instructions to configure the **Manager Security** role:

1. Navigate to the **Core Records** tab in the **Manager Security** role.

2. Clear all privileges from the **Opportunity** and **Document** location entities.

3. Navigate to the **Marketing** tab and clear all privileges from the **Campaign** and **Marketing** list entities.

4. Navigate to the **Sales** tab and clear all privileges from all sales module entities, as shown in the following screenshot:

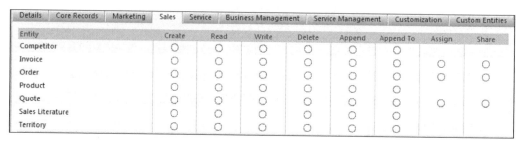

5. Navigate to the **Service** tab and clear all privileges from all service module entities.

6. Click on **Save and Close**.

Follow all the preceding steps to remove the same privileges from the **Recruiter** role as well.

Setting field-level security in Microsoft CRM 2011

Microsoft CRM 2011 contains an OOB feature for field-level security. Using field-level security, we can protect Microsoft CRM form fields from unauthorized access. This feature is only available in custom attributes. You can only apply field-level security to the custom fields of system entities. While creating/modifying fields, you can enable field-level security. The following screenshot shows how we can **Enable/Disable** the **Field Security** option:

Once field-level security is enabled, we can set the field-level security profile. Let's apply field-level security in the offered package section in the **Candidate** entity. We have already enabled field-level security for these three fields under the offered package section in **Candidate** entity. Use the following steps to set the field-level security profile:

1. Navigate to **Settings | Administration | Field Security Profiles**.

2. Click on **New** to create the new security profile.

3. Fill in the following information:

   ○ **Name:** Recruitment Team Profile

   ○ **Description:** Security profile for recruitment team

4. Click on **Save**.

5. Navigate to **Users**, under the **Members** section, in the left-hand navigation.

6. Click on **Add** to add a user from whom you want to secure these fields.

7. Navigate to **Field Permission** under the **Common** section in the left-hand navigation.

8. Select all **records** and click on the **Edit** button.

9. Select **No** from all drop-down fields. These fields can be implemented as shown in the following screenshot:

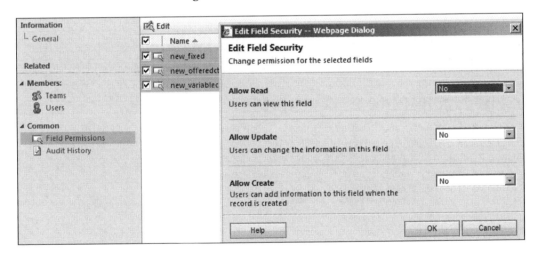

Now all Microsoft CRM users with the **Recruitment** security role won't be able to see the values in these fields. They won't even be able to set values for these fields.

Processes in Microsoft CRM 2011

In Microsoft CRM 2011, the workflow is called the process, and it supports Windows Workflow Foundation. A process is a way to implement business logic using the OOB process designer tool. In Microsoft CRM 2011, we have two categories:

- Dialog
- Workflow

Dialogs

Microsoft CRM 2011 has introduced a new interactive process called **Dialogs**, where we can take input from users and provide results based on the input value. **Dialogs** works in a synchronous manner. We have the following two options to run dialogs:

- As an on-demand process: This option is used when we want to start the process manually on the selected record, using the **Start Dialog** button in the ribbon toolbar.

- As a child process: This option is used when we want to start a process from another process. You can't start a child process directly.

Input arguments and variables

Input arguments are used to pass information from a parent dialog to a child dialog. You can only use input arguments with child dialogs. Thus, we can't add input arguments in a dialog that is configured to run as on-demand.

Variables are used to hold temporary value during dialog lifetime.

Steps

Like workflows, dialogs also contain steps that we can use to design the dialog process. Refer to the following screenshot:

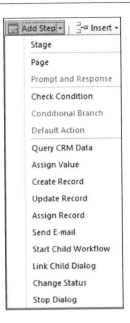

We have the following steps available in the Dialog Designer as shown in the preceding screenshot:

- **Stage**: This step is used to group steps
- **Page**: This step is the interface that is presented to the user
- **Prompt and Response**: Prompts are the questions that are presented to the user, and responses are where answers to those questions are captured
- **Check Condition**: This step is used to check the condition before running the next step
- **Conditional Branch**: This step is used to branch multiple conditions together
- **Default Action**: This step is used to specify the otherwise action
- **Query CRM Data**: This step is used to query Microsoft CRM's existing data
- **Assign Value**: This step is used to assign a value to the input argument or variables
- **Create Record**: This step is used to create an entity record
- **Update Record**: This step is used to update an existing record
- **Assign Record**: This step is used to change the owner of an entity record

- **Send E-mail**: This step is used to send an e-mail
- **Start Child Workflow**: This step is used to used to initiate a child workflow
- **Link Child Dialog**: This step is used to used to link child dialog with current dialog
- **Change Status**: This step is used to change the status of a record
- **Stop Dialog**: This step is used to stop the dialog

Let's create a dialog to get salary information from the candidate. Use the following instructions to create this dialog:

1. Navigate to **Configuration | Process Center | Process**.
2. Click on **New** to create new dialog.
3. Fill the following information:
   - **Process Name: Get Candidate Information**
   - **Entity: Candidate**
   - **Category: Dialog**
   - **Type: New Blank Process**
4. Elect to run the process as an on-demand process.
5. Add a new **Stage** step from the **Add Step** list and label it with `Get Information From User`.
6. Highlight the **Stage** step and select the **Page** step from the **Add Step** list.
7. Enter `Page to Get user Information` in the **Page Label** field.
8. Highlight the **Page** step and select the **Prompt and Response** option from **Add Step list**.
9. Enter `Get Current CTC` in the **Prompt and Response** label and click on **Set Properties**.
10. Enter `May I know your Current CTC` and add values for **Salutation** and **First Name** from **Candidate** entity using **Dynamic Values** section under **Form Assistant**.
11. Select `Single Line` for **Response Type**.
12. Select `Float` for **Data Type**.
13. Click on **Save and Close**.

The following screenshot is of a **Prompt and Response** dialog:

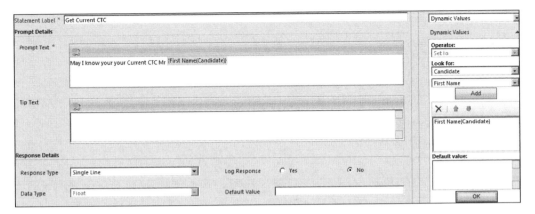

We need to create a prompt for our dialog variable, so we create the **Prompt and Response** dialog using the following steps:

1. To get the expected CTC, we set the following variables:
   - **Statement Label**: Get Expected CTC
   - **Prompt Text**: What is your Expected CTC
   - **Response Type**: Single Line
   - **Data Type:** Float

2. To check whether relocation is required or not:
   - **Statement Label**: Relocation Required
   - **Prompt Text:** Do you need Relocation
   - **Response Type: Optionset** (picklist)
   - **Data Type: Integer**
   - **Provide Values**: **Define values**
   - Add two values:

     Label: Yes, **Value:** 100,000,000

     Label: No, **Value:** 100,000,001

> As we need to use these values to update the candidate entity record, the value of the **Optionset** item should match the values of **Optionset** in the condition entity for that attribute.

3. To get the notice period:
    ○ **Statement Label**: Notice Period
    ○ **Prompt Text**: What is your notice period
    ○ **Response Type**: Single Line
    ○ **Data Type**: Text

After setting all variables for **Prompt and Response**, our stage should look like the following screenshot:

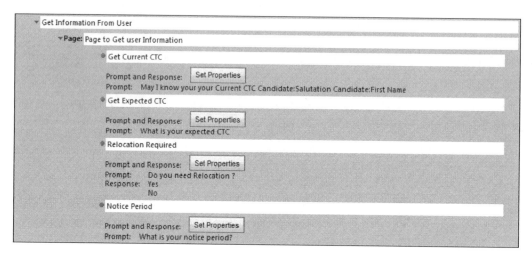

Now that we have collected all variable information, let's create steps to update the candidate entity record. Use the following steps to create an updated candidate record:

1. Add a new stage using **Add Step.**
2. Enter Update Candidate record with variable values in **Stage label** field.
3. Select the **Stage** step and add the **Update step** option from the **Add Step** list.
4. Click on **Set Properties.**
5. Select the **Current CTC** field and select **Get Current CTC** from the **Look for** dropdown.
6. Click on the **Add** button and on **OK** to set response text in the **Current CTC** field.
7. Follow the preceding steps to set all variable values in their respective fields.

After setting variable response text for the fields, the **Current Salary Information** section should look like the following screenshot:

8. Add the **Change Status** step from **Add Step**.

9. Set **Status** to Contacted.

10. Activate dialog using the **Activity** button from the toolbar.

Now that our dialog is ready, we need to activate it; click on **Activate** on the dialog toolbar.

Workflows

Workflows enable you to automate the business process. We can run workflows for multiple entities or a specific entity. OOB Workflow Designer provides us with the functionality to apply different checks before executing any sequence. We can initiate a workflow using different options; it could be an on-demand workflow that we can start manually or we can set a workflow to run automatically based on a specific action. We can also use the workflow as a child workflow of another workflow.

 You can also execute workflows through JavaScript and server-side code.

Execution of workflows is dependent on an asynchronous service; this service is used by Microsoft CRM to execute long-running operations. So, we need to make sure this service is up and running if we are going to implement workflows.

To start a workflow, we can make any one of the following selections:

We can configure workflows to start when:

- **Record is created**: This option is used to run workflows when a new record is created

- **Record status changes**: This option is used to run workflows when the record state changes, for example, when a record is activated or deactivated

- **Record is assigned**: This option is used when the owner of the record is changed

- **Record fields change**: This option is used when the value of the selected fields is changed

- **Record is deleted**: This option is used when the record is deleted

Workflow scope

Workflow scope defines the level of records that a workflow can effect; it is similar to access levels. You can define user scope when you want to run workflows on records owned by a user, but if an organization level is set, any record can trigger a workflow.

The workflow scope levels are shown in the following screenshot:

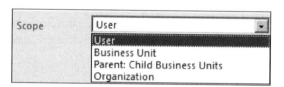

We have the following options to set workflow scope:

- **User**: If workflow scope is set to **User** and is set to run when an entity record is created, the workflow will only be executed if the owner of the workflow creates a record.

- **Business Unit**: When workflow scope is set to **Business Unit** and is set to run when an entity record is created, the workflow will execute when any user from the same business unit of the workflow owner creates an entity record.

- **Parent: Child Business Units**: When workflow scope is set to **Parent: Child Business Unit** and is set to run when an entity record is created, the workflow will be executed when any user from the same business unit and from all the subordinate business units of the workflow owner create an entity record.

- **Organization**: If workflow scope is set to **Organization** and is set to run when an entity record is created, it will be executed when any user creates an entity record.

When an automatic workflow is initiated, the security of the workflow owner is enforced, but when an on-demand workflow is initiated, the security of the current user is enforced to run the workflow.

Workflow steps

You can use different steps available in the workflow step editor based on our requirements. We can divide workflow steps into three sections, which we will look at now.

Check condition

We can apply a check condition to fields to initiate a specific action based on the condition. For example, let's say we want to check whether a candidate is promoted to the HR round or not. We can apply a check condition to the **Promoted to HR Round** field to check its value, as shown in the following screenshot:

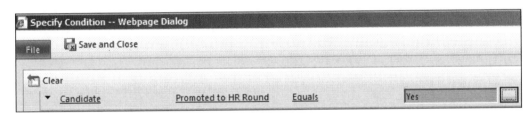

We can also use a condition branch if we want to check different conditions.

Wait condition

We can use a wait condition when we have to pause a process until some conditions are met.

Actions

The workflow steps editor provides the following options to perform different actions:

- **Create Record**: This option is used to create a new record
- **Update Record**: This option is used to update an existing record

- **Assign Record**: This option is used to assign a new owner; it could be a team or a user
- **Send E-mail**: This option is used to send e-mail notifications
- **Start Child Workflow**: Using this option, we can initiate a workflow that is configured to run as a child workflow
- **Change Status**: This option is used to change the status of Microsoft CRM records
- **Stop Workflow**: We can use this option if we want to stop workflow execution

We can also extend workflow steps by writing a custom workflow.

Now that we have a basic understanding of a workflow, let's create the workflow required for our application. We will create a workflow to generate tasks for a recruiter who is working on candidate records. We need to create the following workflows:

- Workflow to generate a phone call to get salary information from a candidate
- Workflow to generate tasks to arrange a technical panel and set an appointment
- Workflow to generate tasks based on different interview feedback

Use the following steps to create our workflows:

1. Navigate to **Configuration | Process Center | Process**.
2. Click on **New** to create a workflow.
3. Fill the following information in the workflow properties:
    - **Process name**: `Generate Phone Call to get Salary Details`
    - **Entity**: **Candidate**
    - **Category**: **Workflow**
    - **Type**: **New blank process**
4. Set the following properties for the workflow:
    - **Scope: Organization**
    - **Start when: Record is Created**
5. Add the **Create Record** step from **Add Step**.
6. Set `Create Phone Call` as the **Create Record** step label.
7. Select the **Phone Call** entity from **Create Dropdown** and click on the **Set Properties** button.

8. Fill the following information in the **Task** window:

   ° **Subject**: Regarding Candidate hiring process

   ° **Description**: Please contact candidate to get salary information, Please run "Get Candidate Information" dialog. Please make sure to ask for the availability of candidate for technical interview

   ° Click on the **Owner** field and select **Candidate** as the owner from the **Look for:** section under **Dynamics Values** from **Form Assistant**

   ° Set **Candidate Mobile Number** from **Look for:** under **Dynamic values** to **Mobile Number**

   ° Click on **Save and Close** to see the following form:

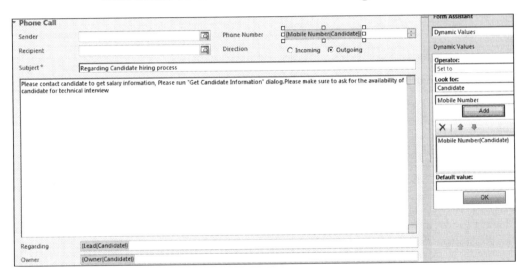

9. Click on **Activate** to activate the process.

Use the following steps to create a workflow to generate tasks at different levels based on interview feedback:

1. Navigate to **Configuration** | **Process Center** | **Process and Select New to create a workflow.**

2. Fill the following information in the workflow properties:

   ° **Process name**: Arrange Technical Panel and set appointment

   ° **Entity**: **Candidate**

   ° **Category**: **Workflow**

   ° **Type**: **New blank process**

3. Set the following properties for the workflow:
   - **Scope**: **Organization**
   - **Start when**: **Record field change**
   - Select the **Promoted to PM Round, Promoted to HR Round,** and **Hired fields** from the **field selection** window

4. Add **Check Condition** steps.

5. Configure **Check Condition** to check whether the value for the **Promoted to PM Round** field is **Yes**.

6. Add the **Create** step to create tasks from the **Add step** list.

7. Enter `Create task to arrange PM and schedule interview` in the **Create** label.

8. Select the **Task** entity from the **Create** dropdown and click on **Set Properties**.

9. Fill the following information in the **Task** window:
   - **Subject**: `Regarding Candidate hiring process`
   - **Task Description**: `Candidate is selected in technical round, Please arrange PM and schedule PM round`
   - Click on the **Owner field** and select the **Candidate owner** from the **Look for:** section under **Dynamics Values** from **Form Assistant**
   - Click on **Save and Close**

We have added steps in our workflow to create a task for when a candidate is selected in the technical round. Now we need to add a condition in our workflow to check whether the PM round has been cleared; then, we need to create a task to set the HR round. Otherwise we need to set the status of the candidate to disqualify. Use the following steps to add a task for the HR round in the same workflow:

1. Add the **Conditional Branch** step to check if **Promoted to PM Round** is equal to **No**.

2. Add the **Change Status** step under **Conditional Branch** and set status to **Disqualify**.

3. Add **Check Condition** step.

4. Configure **Check Condition** to check whether the value of the **Promoted to HR Round** field is **Yes**.

5. Add the **Create step** to create a task from the **Add step** list.

6. Enter `Create task to arrange HR manager and schedule interview` in the **Create label.**

7. Select the **Task** entity from the **Create** dropdown and click on **Set Properties**.

8. Fill the following information in the **Task** window:
   - **Subject**: `Regarding Candidate hiring process`
   - **Task Description**: `Candidate cleared PM round, Please arrange HR manager and schedule HR round`
   - Click on the **Owner field** and select the **Candidate owner** from **Form assistant | Dynamics Values | Look for:**

9. Click on **Save and Close**.

10. Add the **Conditional Branch** step to check if **Promoted to HR Round** is equal to **No**.

11. Add the **Change Status** step under **Conditional Branch** and set status to **Disqualify**.

Now we need to add a condition in our workflow to check whether the candidate is hired or not; if the candidate is hired, we need to add a task to prepare an offer letter for the candidate.

1. Add the **Check Condition** step.

2. Configure the **Check Condition** step to check whether the value of the **Hired** field is equal to **Yes**.

3. Add the **Create** step to create a task from the **Add step** list.

4. Enter `Create task to prepare Offer letter` in the **Create** label.

5. Select the **Task** entity from the **Create** dropdown and click on **Set Properties**.

6. Fill the following information in the **Task** window:
   - **Subject:** `Regarding Candidate hiring process`
   - **Task Description:** `Candidate clear HR round Please release offer letter`
   - Click on the **Owner field** and **select Candidate HR Manager** from **Form assistant | Dynamics Values | Look for:**

7. Click on **Save and Close**.

8. Add the **Conditional Branch** step to check if the **Hired** value is equal to **No**.

9. Add the **Change Status** step under **Conditional Branch** and set the status to **Disqualify**.

10. After adding all these steps, our stage should look like the following screenshot:

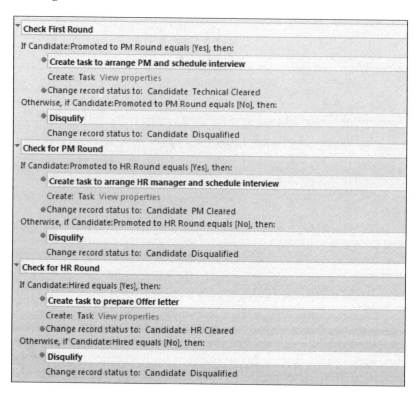

We need to activate the workflow by selecting **Activate** from the workflow toolbar.

Now our Employee Recruitment Management System is ready to use. We need to add a CRM user who will be using Microsoft CRM and need to assign an appropriate role to them.

Importing data in Microsoft CRM 2011

The recruiter team has selected some candidates from a job site and downloaded their resumes; we need to import these candidate records into Microsoft CRM with their resume as an attachment. In order to import data into Microsoft CRM, we need to first download the data import template for the **Candidate** and **Note** entities.

 You can refer to *Chapter 2, Customizing Microsoft Dynamics CRM 2011*, to export the data import template from Microsoft CRM.

Use the following steps to import a resume to Microsoft CRM:

1. Copy `Candidate.xml` into a new folder, let's say `DataImport`.
2. Create a folder called `Attachments` under `DataImport`, and keep all resumes in that folder.
3. Fill the required information in `Note.xml`.
4. Select all files from the `Attachments` folder and zip them.

The `Note.xml` document should look like the following screenshot. The value of the relevant column should match with the exact format, such as *First name(Space) Last name*.

For example, if we are going to import data for a candidate whose first name is Mohan and last name is Mishra, the value of the corresponding field should be "Mohan Mishra".

We need to make sure you don't have duplicate candidate records in Microsoft CRM 2011 (candidates with the same first name and last name), otherwise the import will fail. In that case, we can map the corresponding fields using the candidate record **GUID**.

Title	Owner	File Name	Description	Regarding	Document
Resume	Amit Kumar	Mohan.docx		Mohan Mis	Mohan.docx
Resume	Amit Kumar	Shila.docx		Shila Sharr	Shila.docx
Resume	Amit Kumar	Anita.docx		Anita Mada	Anita.docx
Resume	Amit Kumar	Kundan.docx		Kundan Kur	Kundan.docx
Resume	Amit Kumar	Meena.docx		Meena Nag	Meena.docx
Resume	Amit Kumar	Neelam.docx		Neelam Gul	Neelam.docx

> You need to add the **Regarding** and **Document** columns in `Note.xml`; they won't originally be there in the downloaded `Note.xml` template.

Once all the files are ready the **DataImport** folder looks like the following screenshot:

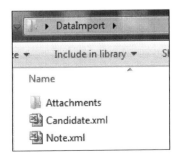

Select all these files and zip them. Once the `.zip` file is ready, we can import this file in Microsoft CRM 2011 using the OOB import wizard. The Microsoft CRM 2011 data import wizard will pick automatic mapping to import data in the **Candidate** and **Note** entities.

Testing Employee Recruitment Management System

As soon as data is imported in Microsoft CRM, our workflow will start executing and will create phone calls associated with every candidate record imported in Microsoft CRM. The recruiter can start working on candidate records one by one. When the recruiter checks this activity, he will find corresponding phone calls to every candidate record, as shown in the following screenshot:

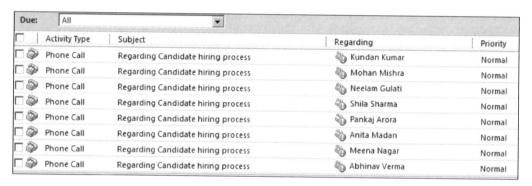

	Activity Type	Subject	Regarding	Priority
	Phone Call	Regarding Candidate hiring process	Kundan Kumar	Normal
	Phone Call	Regarding Candidate hiring process	Mohan Mishra	Normal
	Phone Call	Regarding Candidate hiring process	Neelam Gulati	Normal
	Phone Call	Regarding Candidate hiring process	Shila Sharma	Normal
	Phone Call	Regarding Candidate hiring process	Pankaj Arora	Normal
	Phone Call	Regarding Candidate hiring process	Anita Madan	Normal
	Phone Call	Regarding Candidate hiring process	Meena Nagar	Normal
	Phone Call	Regarding Candidate hiring process	Abhinav Verma	Normal

Once the recruiter has started calling candidates one by one, he will receive a prompt question for the candidate and will get a response from the candidate. Once the dialog execution is finished, it will update the candidate records and will change their status to **Contacted**, which will again initiate a workflow, which in turn creates a task for the recruiter to schedule the technical round. The **Prompt and Response** dialog will be as follows:

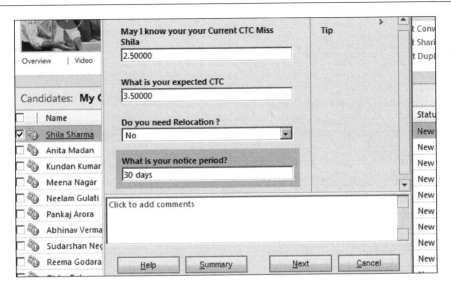

The recruiter will create an appointment to schedule an interview when both candidate and interviewer are available. Once the technical round is completed, the interviewer will promote the candidate to the PM round and a workflow will start, which will change the candidate status to **Technical Clear** and will create a task for the recruiter to schedule the PM round. The recruiter will then arrange for the PM round and will update the candidate about the interview status. Once the PM round is cleared, the workflow will create another task to arrange an HR interview, and once the HR round is clear, a new task will be created for the HR manger to release the offer letter to the candidate. Once the candidate is hired, the recruiter will convert the candidate record into an employee record using the **Qualify** ribbon button from the Candidate toolbar.

Summary

In this chapter, we learned how we can leverage Microsoft CRM 2011 to build an employee recruitment application. We learned how to customize Microsoft CRM 2011 to fit our business-specific requirements, to create new fields and customize entity forms, and also to apply field-level security in Microsoft CRM 2011. Then we learned about relationships in Microsoft CRM 2011, how we can import data in Microsoft CRM 2011 with attachments, and how we can use a process to automate business activities. Finally, we learned about dialogs and workflows.

In the next chapter, we will show you how we can use Microsoft CRM 2011 to automate a hotel management system.

4
Implementing Business Logic through Plugins

In this chapter, we are going to use Microsoft Dynamics CRM 2011 to build a hotel management application. We will learn how to create a Custom entity and how to use a plugin to implement business logic for our hotel management application. In this chapter, we will learn how we can use the developers' toolkit that comes with CRM SDK, to make our plugin development easy.

In this chapter we are going to discuss the following topics:

- Application scope
- Hotel management system design
- Data model for a hotel management system
- Customizing and configuring Microsoft CRM 2011 using sub-grids
- Setting up a product in Microsoft CRM 2011
- Understanding plugins in MS CRM 2011

Application scope

We are going to use Microsoft CRM 2011 to develop a hotel management sample application. In our sample application, we will use some of the Microsoft CRM 2011 OOB entities. We will also create some new entities to store room and food item details. We will utilize the product catalog of Microsoft CRM 2011 to store the room's category, and we will utilize the OOB Price List entity to store pricing information for rooms. We are going to use the Microsoft CRM 2011 on-premise installation on a single server for our application.

Hotel Management System Design

In our sample application, we are going to implement a hotel booking system. The following flow diagram shows the process for the booking system used in our application. When a customer arrives, the front desk executive will enquire for a room type based on the customer's choice. If the room is available, the front desk executive will create a customer record in the application, assign a room to the customer, and set the check-in and check-out dates. On the check-out date, a bill will be created for the customer, and the room will be free.

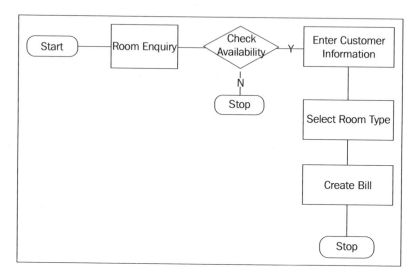

In our sample application, we will be using the following main entities:

Sr. No.	Entity	Description
1	Account	This is used to store hotel information
2	Contact	This is used to store customer information
3	Product	This is used to store the room's category
4	Unit group	This is used to store the primary unit
5	Price list	This is used to store price information for the room category
6	Invoice	This is used to store bill information for the customer
7	Room	This is the Custom entity to store a room's record
8	Food	This is the Custom entity used to store food items

Data model for a hotel management system

In the next section, we will see the main entity data model that we are going to use in our sample hotel management application. We have used some OOB entities without any customization, so we have not provided the data model for those entities, such as the price list and unit group. Refer to *Appendix B, Hotel Management Data Model and Design*, for hotel management system data model.

Customizing and configuring Microsoft CRM 2011 using sub-grids

We need to customize and configure Microsoft CRM 2011 according to our sample application. We need to perform the following steps to customize Microsoft CRM 2011.

Customizing MS CRM 2011 entities

We need to customize the existing entities based on the data model. Refer to *Appendix B, Hotel Management Data Model and Design*, for more information. We need to create new Room and Food entities.

First, we need to create our Solution and include all the required entities in that Solution. Please refer to the previous chapters to create a Solution. Once we have our Solution, we need to customize the OOB entity fields. We also need to rename the entities and their views.

As we have already discussed how to rename entities and their views, we are not going to look at it again here. Please refer to *Chapter 2, Customizing Microsoft Dynamics CRM 2011*, for more on this type of customization.

While creating a new entity, we need to consider the points explained in the following sections.

Custom prefix

In Microsoft CRM 2011, we can use the custom prefix for our Custom entity and custom attributes. Using the custom prefix is important if you have an ISV partner; it will ensure that nobody creates an entity with the same name. You can use the custom prefix by modifying the default publisher, or you can create a new publisher with the custom prefix. Perform the following steps to modify the default publisher's prefix:

1. Navigate to **Settings | Customizations | Publishers**.
2. Select the default publisher from the list.
3. Modify the **Prefix** field and change it to your custom prefix, and click on **Save and Close**.

Set the prefix name for custom entities and fields	
Prefix *	new
Name Preview	new_entity

4. Navigate to **Settings | Solutions**, and click on **Publish All Customizations**.

Entity ownership

While creating the Custom entity, we can define entity ownership. **Entity ownership** defines the type of operations that can be performed on that entity record. We have the following options to set ownership:

Ownership	Description
Organization	Organization-owned entities are accessible to the whole organization, so it is not possible to share and assign organization-owned entity records.
User or Team	These entities can be owned either by individual users or by teams. These entities can be shared and assigned to other users or teams. Security is applied according to the business unit with which the current owner is associated.

Options for an entity

While creating a new Custom entity, we have different options to set for the **Communication & Collaboration, Data Services**, and **Outlook & Mobile** fields. We can set the following options for these fields:

Option	Description
Notes	This is used to create a relationship with the Annotation entity. If this option is selected, it adds a Notes control in the entity form where we attach notes to the current entity record. We can also upload an attachment using this option.

Option	Description
Activities	This option is used to create a relationship with Activities entity.
Connections	We can select this option if we want to connect the current entity record with other entities.
Sending e-mail	We can select this option if we want to add the Send Direct E-mail button on the entity ribbon.
Mail merge	If this option is selected, we can use this entity to merge e-mails.
Document management	If this option is selected, we can track a document on SharePoint related to the current entity record.
Queues	If this option is selected, this entity can be used in queues.
Duplicate detection	If this option is selected, we can detect the duplicate record for this entity.
Auditing	If this option is selected, we can track changes in entity records.
Mobile express	If this option is selected, we can use this entity in Mobile Express.
Reading pane in CRM for Microsoft Outlook	If this option is selected, records of this entity will be displayed in the reading pane in Microsoft CRM 2011 for Outlook
Offline capability for CRM for Microsoft Outlook	If this option is selected, we can use this entity while in offline mode in Microsoft CRM 2011 for Outlook.

Let's create our Room and Food entities; perform the following steps to create the Room entity:

1. Navigate to **Settings | Solutions** and open the `Development` Solution (we have created a new Solution named `Development`).

2. Navigate to **Entities** under **Components**.

3. Click on **New** from the entity ribbon:

4. Enter the following information to create an entity:

General tab	
Display Name	Room
Name	This will be configured automatically and will be referred using SDK
Ownership	User or Team
Areas that display this entity	Settings
Communication & Collaboration	Just select Connections and Duplicate detection for this field
Primary field tab	
Display Name	Room no
Name	This will be configured automatically

 While we are working with SOAP endpoints in Microsoft CRM 2011, we need to use the field's logical name, but while working with REST endpoints, we need to use the schema name of the field.

5. Click on **Save** to save the entity.

6. Now we need to add new fields for the Room entity based on the previous data model.

Please follow the preceding steps to create the Food entity, and enter the following information for entity properties:

General tab	
Display Name	Food
Name	This will be configured automatically
Ownership	Organization
Areas that display this entity	Settings
Communication & Collaboration	Just select Duplicate detection
Primary field tab	
Keep the primary tab fields as default	

Customizing entity forms

After customizing entities' attributes based on our data models, let us customize our Custom entity forms.

We need to remove any unwanted fields from the entity form; we can just select the attribute and the remove button from the entity form ribbon to remove the fields from the entity form. The MS CRM entity form contains some fields that are in a locked state. But even if we don't want to use these fields, we can't remove them using supported methods. But we can hide those fields. Perform the following steps to hide the unwanted sections and fields from the entity fields:

1. Open the entity form to customize it.

2. Double-click on the field/section that we want to hide.

3. Unselect the **Visible by default** checkbox in the **Visibility** section under the **Display** tab:

After removing and hiding the unwanted fields and sections, we also need to remove the unwanted left navigation section from the entity forms. Please refer to the previous chapters for how to remove unwanted left navigation items from entity forms.

Hotel entity form design

Once we have completed the previously mentioned changes, our entity forms should look like the following screenshot:

▼ **General**		
Hotel Name *		Main Phone
E-mail		Other Phone
Web Site		Fax
Address		
Street 1		City
Street 2		State/Province
Street 3		ZIP/Postal Code
Country/Region		Phone

Room entity design

Our Room entity form fields should look like the following screenshot:

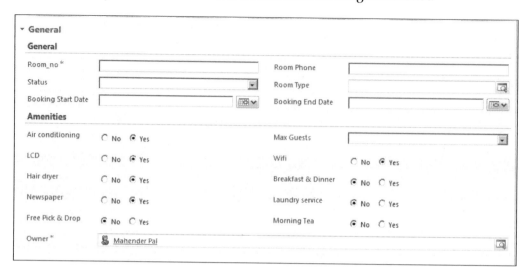

Customer entity design

We need to modify our Customer entity form as in the following screenshot:

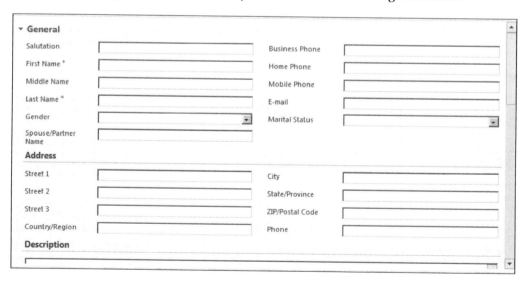

Bill entity design

The Invoice entity contains many address fields for shipping and billing information, which are not required for our application. But as all these fields are in a locked state, we can't remove them from the entity form. But we can hide them using the OOB functionality. So follow the previous steps to hide those unwanted fields and sections.

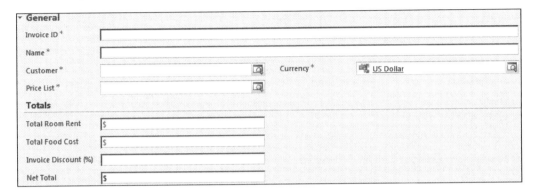

Product entity design

We need to change our Product entity form design as in the following screenshot:

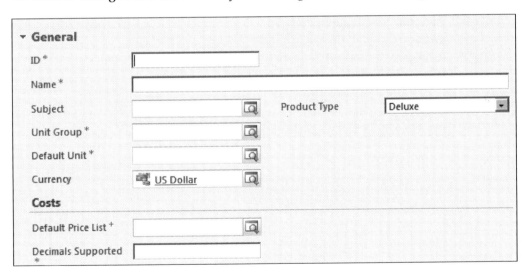

Food entity design

We need to hide the **Name** field from the Food entity; after that our form should look like the following screenshot:

Now we need to change the translation for the OOB entities. Refer *Chapter 2, Customizing Microsoft Dynamics CRM 2011*, to see how to change the translation labels in MS CRM. We need to rename Account to Hotel, Contact to Customer, and Invoice to Bill.

Customizing Microsoft CRM 2011 navigation

We need to customize the MS CRM site map to remove the unwanted left navigation section from the site map. We need to customize the site map based on the following table. Refer to *Chapter 2, Customizing Microsoft Dynamics CRM 2011*, to customize the site map.

Sr. No.	Customization detail
1	Remove the Sales, Marketing, Service, and Resource Center fields from the left navigation section
2	Rename the left navigation; navigate to Workplace	Reservation, and then navigate to Settings	Configurations to rename the left navigation
3	Create a navigation item for the Hotel, Customer, Bill, and Room entities (we can add/remove these items using SiteMap Editor easily)

After customizing the site map, MS CRM UI should look like the following screenshot:

Using sub-grids

Microsoft CRM 2011 has new features to show an associated view in the entity form called **sub-grid**. In MS CRM 4.0, we used IFRAME to show an associated view in the entity form. But now, using just view-click we can add a sub-grid in the entity form. It is important to note that sub-grids are not associated views. A sub-grid allows us to filter a record set based on the data source selected to view the data. We can set the following data source for the sub-grid:

- **Records**: We can select this option if we want to see a related record or all entity records
- **Entity**: This is the name of the entity that we want to see in the sub-grid
- **Default view**: We can select the default view for the sub-grid

We can also set different additional options for the sub-grid:

- **Display search box**: We can select this option if we want to show a search textbox with the view
- **Display index**: We can select this option to display an alphabetical index with the view
- **View selector**: We can select this option if we want to allow the user to select a different view for the sub-grid

Perform the following steps to add a sub-grid on the customer form for food items:

1. Navigate to **Configuration | Solution**.
2. Open the `Development` Solution.
3. Navigate to **Entities | Customer**.
4. Open the Customer entity form.
5. Select the **Insert** tab and add a new section. Let's call it `Food Details`.
6. Select the **Food Details** section and click on **Sub-Grid** under the **Insert** Tab.

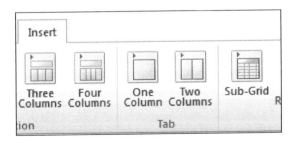

7. Select the sub-grid properties, as shown in the following screenshot:

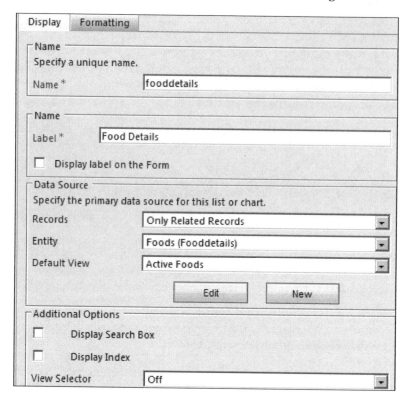

8. Click on **Save and Close**.

9. Publish the Customer entity from the Solution ribbon.

Setting up a product in Microsoft CRM 2011

Microsoft CRM provides OOB product catalog functionality. We can use a product catalog to store the products or services used in an organization. A product can be a physical item or service. We can define the price list based on the product or its services. For setting up a product, we need to perform the following process:

1. Set a unit group.

2. Set a product.

3. Set a price list.

Setting up a unit group

A unit group contains the basic unit in which the product will be available.
For example, kilogram, liter, and hour are all measuring units. So before setting
up the product, we need to set a base unit for the product. Perform the following
steps to set a unit group and primary unit:

1. Navigate to **Configuration | Business | Product Catalog**.

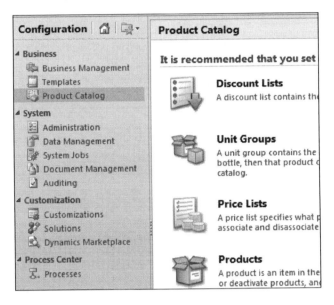

2. Select **Unit Groups**.
3. Select **New** from the **Unit Groups** ribbon toolbar.
4. Enter the following information in the **Create Unit Group** dialog box:
    ◦ **Name**: Service
    ◦ **Primary Unit**: Hour

5. Once the unit group is created, it will open **Service Unit Group Record**.
6. Navigate to **Units** from the **Common** section.
7. Click on the **Add New Unit** button from the **List Unit Tools** group.
8. Enter the following information in the new **Unit** dialog box:
    ◦ **Name**: Day
    ◦ **Quantity**: 8
    ◦ **Base Unit**: Hour

Once we have set up a basic unit group, let's set up our products. We are going to use the products to represent our room service category. We have the following room types:

- Deluxe room
- Deluxe, non-AC room
- Semi-deluxe room
- Four-bed family room
- Economy room

Perform the following steps to set up a product:

1. Navigate to **Configuration** | **Business** | **Product Catalog**.
2. Select **Product**.
3. Click on **New** in the **Room Category** tab to create a new product.
4. Enter the following information:
   - **ID**: Dlx
   - **Name**: Deluxe Room
   - **Subject**: Default subject
   - **Unit Group**: Service
   - **Default Unit**: Day
   - **Currency**: US dollar
   - **Product Type**: Deluxe
   - **Decimals Supported**: 2
5. Click on **Save and Close**.

Follow the preceding steps to set up the following products:

ID	Name	Subject	Unit Group	Default Unit	Product Type	Decimals Supported
Dlx 2	Deluxe Non A/C	Room	Service	Day	Deluxe Non A/C	2
SDlx	Semi Deluxe	Room	Service	Day	Semi Deluxe	2
Fbed	Family Room	Room	Service	Day	Four Bed	2
Eco	Economy Room	Room	Service	Day	Economy	2

Once we have set up the product categories, we need to set up the price list for our product categories.

Setting up a price list

Price lists are a way to manage different pricing value for the same product. Once a price list is created, we can add multiple price list items using multiple products. Perform the following steps to create a price list in MS CRM 2011:

1. Navigate to **Configuration | Business | Price Lists**.
2. Select **New** from the **Price List** group in the ribbon toolbar.
3. Enter `Default` in the **Name** field of the Price List form.
4. Click on the **Save** button.
5. Navigate to **Price List Items** under the **Common** left navigation section.
6. Click on **Add New Price List Item**.
7. Enter the following information in the Price List item form:
   - **Price List**: Default
   - **Product**: Deluxe
   - **Unit**: Day
   - **Pricing Method**: Currency amount
   - **Amount**: 300
   - **Quantity Selling Option**: No control
8. Click on **Save and Close**.

We need to create price list items for all the room categories. Perform the following steps to set up the price list items:

Sr. No.	Field Name	Value
1	Price List	Deluxe Non A/C
	Unit	Day
	Pricing Method	Currency amount
	Amount	200
	Quantity Selling Option	No control

Sr. No.	Field Name	Value
2	Price List	Semi Deluxe
	Unit	Day
	Pricing Method	Currency amount
	Amount	150
	Quantity Selling Option	No control
3	Price List	Family Room
	Unit	Day
	Pricing Method	Currency amount
	Amount	100
	Quantity Selling Option	No control
4	Price List	Economy
	Unit	Day
	Pricing Method	Currency amount
	Amount	50
	Quantity Selling Option	No control

Understanding plugins in Microsoft CRM 2011

Now we have customized Microsoft CRM 2011, so let's create a plugin to implement our custom business logic. Microsoft CRM 2011 provides us with the functionality to implement our custom business logic in terms of a .NET assembly. We can consume Microsoft CRM APIs in .NET to access Microsoft CRM context information and impose our business logic.

Plugin execution pipeline

We can register a plugin on specific events, and it will execute an event framework based on the message pipeline execution model. We can register the plugin in the following modes:

- Asynchronous mode
- Synchronous mode

So the event pipeline executes a plugin in asynchronous mode or synchronous mode. If the plugin is registered in asynchronous mode, it is queued by Microsoft CRM 2011 Asynchronous Service and executed in background mode at a later time. But on the other hand, if the plugin is registered in synchronous mode, it is executed at that moment only. Asynchronous plugins are best suited for long-running jobs whereas synchronous plugins are best suited for where we need a response immediately. In Microsoft CRM 2011, synchronous plugins are now part of the database transaction, which means that if our plugin is running in synchronous mode and if an exception occurs, it will be passed to the platform. Because of this, the entire transaction will be rolled back to its earlier state. So any registered plugin that is being executed under the database transaction and that passes an exception to the platform cancels the core operation. Apart from a rollback of the core operation, it also cancels the execution of any pre or post event registered plugin, and any workflow that is triggered by the same event that the plugin was registered with.

 Note that an asynchronous plugin runs out of the database transaction.

Plugin events

We can register a plugin to run before or after core platform operations. Pre-event plugins are registered before the core operation and are best suited for the requirements where we want to execute our business logic before the core platform operation. After pre-event, core operation is executed by platform.

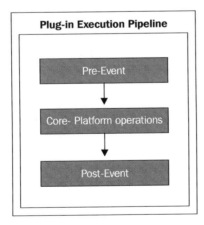

Once the core operation is completed, **Post-Event** is executed. We need to register the plugin to the CRM platform on an entity-specific event. We can get an entity-specific message from message-entity support for the plugins file that comes as a part of CRM SDK.

> Note that you can download the latest SDK of Microsoft CRM 2011 from http://www.microsoft.com/en-us/ download/details.aspx?id=24004.

Plugin security

In order to register a non-isolated plugin, the CRM user should have membership of the deployment administrator group. The deployment administrator group is a special group of Microsoft CRM users who have complete and unrestricted access to perform deployment manager tasks on all the organizations and servers in a Microsoft CRM deployment.

> Only the System Administrator user account or any user account included in the Deployment Administrators' group can run Deployment Manager.

In order to register a plugin, the current Microsoft CRM user should have the following privileges:

- `prvCreatePluginAssembly`
- `prvCreatePluginType`
- `prvCreateSdkMessageProcessingStep`
- `preCreateSdkMessageProcessingStepImage`
- `prvCreateSdkMessageProcessingStepSecureConfig`

To register a plugin in sandbox mode, the current Microsoft CRM user must have the System Administrator role, but membership of the Deployment Administrator group is not required.

> Note that Microsoft Dynamics CRM 2011 supports the execution of plugins in an isolated environment (sandbox). In this isolated environment, a plugin can make use of the full power of the Microsoft Dynamics CRM SDK to access the organization web service, but access to other resources such as the filesystem, system event log, certain network protocols, and registry is not allowed in the sandbox. To get more details on sandbox mode, visit http:// msdn.microsoft.com/en-us/library/gg334752.aspx.

CRM assemblies

While developing the plugin we need to add a reference of MS CRM 2011 plugin assemblies. These assemblies comes as part of the Microsoft CRM 2011 SDK. The following screenshot shows the main assemblies used in a plugin project:

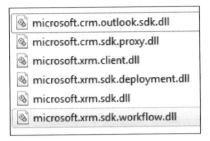

IPluginExecutionContext

IPluginexecutioncontext is a way to get contextual information passed to a plugin during execution time. It contains information such as calling user information, execution pipeline, and entity message on which plugin executes, and entity input/output property bag and so on.

Pre/Post-entity images

Pre and post-entity images are a snapshot of the entity before and after core platform operations respectively. While registering a plugin, we can register images and define a set of attributes that we want to be part of the plugin image.

 You cannot register a pre-entity image for the Create plugin and posting images for the Delete plugin.

We can write the plugin assembly in Visual Studio using C# or VB.NET. We are going to use C# for our plugin sample code and then can register it using Plugin Registration Tool, or through code. Microsoft CRM 2011 also provides a developer toolkit to make MS CRM development easy, so we are going to see how to use **Developer Toolkit** to develop and deploy plugins.

 Note that Developer Toolkit can be found under `\sdk\tools\developertoolkit`.

Writing plugins using Developer Toolkit

Let's write our first business logic. We are going to write a very simple plugin on our Food entity. We are not using a name (default primary) for the Food entity. We will set the selected menu item text and its cost in the **Name** field on creation of the Food entity, so that the customer will have an idea of what they ordered and how much it cost them.

We need to write a function to fetch option set field's text value based on its index value. We can get a value selected by the option set from the entity input property bag.

Perform the following steps to create a plugin package for our application:

1. Open Visual Studio 2010.
2. Navigate to **File | New Project**.
3. Select **Dynamics CRM 2011 Package**.
4. Name it as HotelManagementSystem_Plugins.

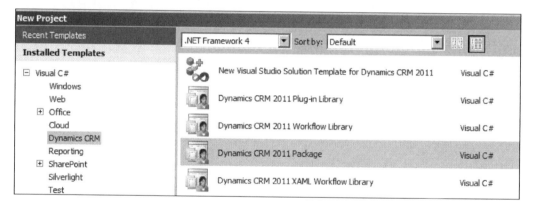

5. You will get a prompt dialog box to enter information to connect to the CRM server, such as the server name and port, authentication to connect to the CRM server.

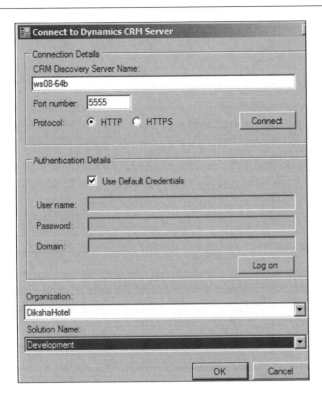

We are using default credentials to connect to the CRM server. If you don't want to use default credentials, you can uncheck this checkbox and enter different user credentials.

6. Right-click on **Project Solution** under **Solution Explorer** and navigate to **Add | New Project**.

7. Select **MS CRM 2011 Plug-in Library** and name it PluginAssemblies, and click on **OK**.

We have created a plugin assembly project. We now need to add a plugin to our entity. Perform the following steps to add a plugin to the Food entity:

1. Right-click on **PluginAssemblies** and select **Properties**.

2. Go to the **Signing** tab, select the **Sign the assembly** checkbox, and close the property dialog box.

3. Navigate to the **View** menu and select **CRM Explorer** if it is not already visible.

4. Expand **Entities** under **CRM Explorer**.

5. Right-click on the **Food** entity and select **Create Plug-in**; Visual Studio will prompt a dialog box to enter the following plugin registration information:

    ○ **Message**: This field contains the description about the event on which we want to trigger our plugin

    ○ **Run in Context**: This is the system account that will own the data changes made by the plugin

    ○ **Pipeline Stage**: The pipeline in which the plugin will run

    ○ **Execution Mode**: The plugin will run in asynchronous or synchronous mode

    ○ **Class**: This is the name of the class file for the plugin

    ○ **Secondary Entity**: It is used when a plugin is triggered for an event requiring two entities like those of the **SetRelated** message

    ○ **Filtering Attributes**: We can select entity attributes; changing those will cause the plugin to be executed

    ○ **Execution Order**: If we have two plugins registered on the same event, we can specify their rank, which should fire first

    ○ **Deployment**: This field defines where we want to deploy the plugin; we have options, such as on the server, on the Microsoft Dynamics CRM for Outlook with offline access, or both

    ○ **Description**: This field gives a description about the plugin

6. We need to select the following information in the **Create Plug-in** dialog box:

    ○ **Message**: **Create**

    ○ **Pipeline**: **Pre-Operation**

    Keep all the other options as default.

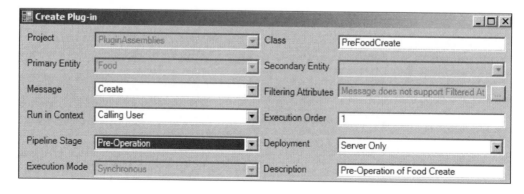

After we have added the plugin, a `PreFoodCreate.cs` file will be created. Double-click on `PreFoodCreate.cs` to edit it. We will get the following code that is generated by Developers Toolkit. We need to edit this file to implement our business logic. This is a common code developed by the toolkit. Common code will be changed accordingly based on the event registration information entered by us.

```
namespaceHotelManagementSystem_Plugins.PluginAssemblies
{
using System;
usingSystem.ServiceModel;
usingMicrosoft.Xrm.Sdk;
usingMicrosoft.Xrm.Sdk.Messages;
usingMicrosoft.Xrm.Sdk.Metadata;
publicclassPreFoodCreate : Plugin
    {
publicPreFoodCreate()
            : base(typeof(PreFoodCreate))
        {
base.RegisteredEvents.Add(newTuple<int, string, string,
Action<LocalPluginContext>>(20, "Create", "new_food", newAction<LocalP
luginContext>(ExecutePreFoodCreate)));
        }
    }
}
```

Downloading the example code

You can download the example code files for all Packt books you have purchased from your account at `http://www.packtpub.com`. If you purchased this book elsewhere, you can visit `http://www.packtpub.com/support` and register to have the files e-mailed directly to you.

You can register for more events here if this plugin is not specific to an individual entity and message combination. You may also need to update your `RegisterFile.crmregisterin` plugin registration file to reflect any change.

For improved performance, Microsoft Dynamics CRM caches plugin instances.

The plugin's `Execute` method should be written to be stateless, as the constructor is not called for every invocation of the plugin. Also, multiple system threads execute the plugin at the same time. All *per invocation state* information is stored in the context. This means that you should not use global variables in plugins.

```
protectedvoidExecutePreFoodCreate(LocalPluginContextlocalContext)
        {
if (localContext == null)
```

```
                {
    thrownewArgumentNullException("localContext");
                }
    // TODO: Implement your custom Plug-in business logic
            }
```

To implement our business logic, we need the Microsoft CRM service context that we can obtain from the local context. Once we have a context, we can fetch our entity and it's attribute from the entity property bag. In our plugin, we are going to fetch a selected option set value from the new_menu field and also the cost for the food item, to store it in the **Name** field of the Food entity. We need to write another function to retrieve the text of the option set based on its selected value. We need to use the RetrieveAttributeRequest class to retrieve the option set data. Once we have the option set, we can compare the option set's value and get the option set's text. Our function should look as follows:

```
    return _SelectedText;}publicstringRetrieveOptionSetValue(IOrganization
    Service service, stringoptionsetName, intoptionsetValue)
            {
    string _SelectedText  = string.Empty;
    try
                {
    RetrieveAttributeRequest _Request = newRetrieveAttributeRequest
                    {
    EntityLogicalName = "new_food",
    LogicalName = "new_menu",
    RetrieveAsIfPublished = true
                    };
    //Execute Request
    RetrieveAttributeResponse _Response =(RetrieveAttributeResponse)
    service.Execute(_Request);
    PicklistAttributeMetadata _PicklistAttributeMetadata
    =(PicklistAttributeMetadata)_Response.AttributeMetadata;
    OptionMetadata[] OptionsetArry = _PicklistAttributeMetadata.OptionSet.
    Options.ToArray();
    foreach (OptionMetadata _OptionsetinOptionsetArry)
                    {
    if (_Optionset.Value == optionsetValue)
                        {

                        _SelectedText = _Optionset.Label.
    UserLocalizedLabel.Label;
                        }
```

```
                        }
                }
        catch (Exception)
                        {
        throw;
                        }
                }
```

Please check the `PreFoodCreate.cs` file under `Chapter4\Code\` `HotelManagementSystem_Plugins\PluginAssemblies` for full code. We need to create another plugin prior to updating the Food entity. Follow the previous steps to create an Update plugin on the Food entity. We need to use the same code to handle the updated event as well. Please refer to the `PreFoodUpdate.cs` file for full code under the `Chapter 4` folder.

Now our plugin assemblies are ready, so let's register them. Perform the following steps to register the plugin:

1. Right-click on **Solution** and select **Deploy**.

2. It will register the Create and Update plugins on the Food entity.

We can check through CRM Explorer, and it should look like the following screenshot:

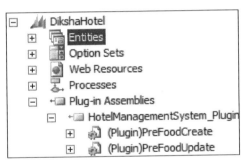

Now we need to write two other plugins for our billing calculation. We need to write the following two plugins on the Bill entity:

- We need a plugin on the Bill Item entity that will calculate the quantity of the bill items based on the check-in and check-out date of customer.

- We need to write a plugin on the Bill entity to calculate the food item bill for the current customer. We also need to calculate the net total based on the cost of the food items and the room rent.

Perform the following steps to create a plugin on the Bill item:

1. Right-click on the **Bill Item** entity on **CRM Explorer** and select **Create Plug-in**.

2. Enter the information shown in the following screenshot in the **Create Plug-in** dialog box:

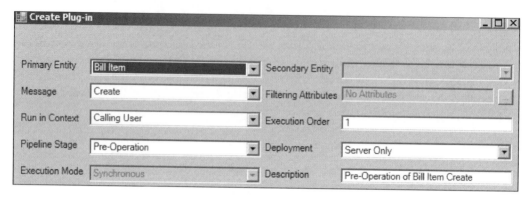

3. Click on **OK** to close the **Create Plug-in** dialog box.

Developer Toolkit will generate the `PreBillItemCreate.cs` file. We can open `PreBillItemCreate.cs` by double-clicking on this file. This file will contain the main function to calculate the number of days based on the current customer's check-in and check-out date. In the following code snippet, we have used the `fetch` query to get check-in and check-out dates. We have used FetchXML to get the check-in and check-out dates for the current customer.

 Note that FetchXML is a query language that is used in Microsoft Dynamics CRM. You can get more details from `http://technet.microsoft.com/en-us/library/gg328332.aspx` on FetchXML.

We need to write another function where the Food Item code of the current invoice customer based on the invoice ID will be fetched. The following function is used to get the number of days:

```
privateintGetNumberofDays(IOrganizationService service, GuidInvoiceId)
        {DateTime _CheckDate = DateTime.MinValue;
DateTime _CheckoutDate = DateTime.MaxValue;
int Duration = 0;
```

```
//get checkin checkout date of the customer based on invoice id
FetchXmlToQueryExpressionRequest Fetch =
newFetchXmlToQueryExpressionRequest();
Fetch.FetchXml = "<fetch version='1.0' output-format='xml-platform'
mapping='logical' distinct='true'>" +
"<entity name='contact'>" +
"<attribute name='new_checkin'/>" +
"<attribute name='new_checkout'/>" +
"<attribute name='contactid'/>" +
"<order attribute='new_checkout' descending='true'/>"+
"<link-entity name='invoice' from='customerid' to='contactid'
alias='aa'>" +
"<filter type='and'>" +
"<condition attribute='invoiceid' operator='eq' uiname='sds'
uitype='invoice' value='" + InvoiceId + "'/>" +
"</filter></link-entity></entity></fetch>";
FetchXmlToQueryExpressionResponseresp =
(FetchXmlToQueryExpressionResponse)service.Execute(Fetch);
QueryExpressionqueryExpression = resp.Query;
EntityCollection result = service.RetrieveMultiple(queryExpression);
if (result.Entities.Count> 0)
            {Entity _Customer = (Entity)result.Entities[0];
if (_Customer.Attributes.Contains("new_checkin") && _Customer.
Attributes.Contains("new_checkout")){
                _CheckDate = ((DateTime)_Customer.Attributes["new_
checkin"]).Date;
                    _CheckoutDate = ((DateTime)_Customer.
Attributes["new_checkout"]).Date;
                    Duration = DateDiff(_CheckDate,_CheckoutDate);
return Duration;}Else{
thrownewInvalidPluginExecutionException("Checkin or Checkout date is
not specified for customer");
                    }}


return Duration;
        }
```

In the preceding code, we have used `InvalidPluginExecutionException`, which is used to show an exception message to the user in Microsoft CRM. Once we have the check-in and check-out date, we can calculate the days' difference between these dates to get the number of days. The following function is used to get the number of days between two passed dates:

```
privateintDateDiff(DateTime Min, DateTime Max)
        {
//get date difference
TimeSpan _TimeSpan = Max - Min;
return _TimeSpan.Days;

        }
```

Please refer to `PreBillItemCreate.cs` under `Chapter4\Code\ HotelManagementSystem_Plugins\PluginAssemblies` for the full code.

We need to write a plugin on the Bill entity to calculate the food item bill based on the current customer. We also need to calculate the net total based on the cost of the food items and the room rent. In the Bill entity, we have created a custom field to store the food cost and room rent amount. Once we have both, we will store the net total in another custom field created in the Bill entity.

Right-click on the **Bill** entity in **CRM Explorer** and select **Create Plug-in**.

We need to fill in the information as shown in the following screenshot:

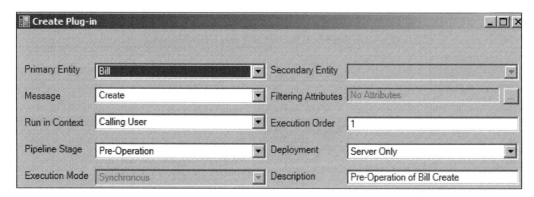

Developer Toolkit will generate a `PreBillCreate.cs` file for us. First we need to get an ID for the current customer; after that, based on the customer ID, we can calculate the total food cost for that customer.

The following function is used to get the calculated value for the total food cost based on the customer ID:

```
privateDecimalGetFoodTotal(Guidcustomerid, IOrganizationService
service)
        {Decimal _Total = 0;
DataCollection<Entity> _Fooditems = null;
try
            {QueryExpression _Query = newQueryExpression{EntityName =
"new_food",
ColumnSet = newColumnSet("new_cost"),
                    Criteria ={
FilterOperator = LogicalOperator.And,
Conditions ={
newConditionExpression{
AttributeName="new_fooddetailsid",
                        Operator=ConditionOperator.Equal,
                        Values={ customerid}
                            }}}};

  _Fooditems = service.RetrieveMultiple(_Query).Entities;
if (_Fooditems.Count> 0)
                {for (inti = 0; i< _Fooditems.Count; i++)
                    {EntityFooditem = (Entity)_Fooditems[i];
if (Fooditem.Attributes.Contains("new_cost")){
                        _Total = _Total + ((Money)Fooditem.
Attributes["new_cost"]).Value;}}}}

catch (Exception Ex)
            {thrownewInvalidPluginExecutionException(Ex.Message);}
return _Total;}
```

In the preceding code, we have used the QueryExpression class, which is used to query Microsoft CRM entities. You can refer to http://technet.microsoft.com/en-us/library/gg334688.aspx for more details on query expression.

Please refer to PreBillCreate.cs under Chapter4\Code\HotelManagementSystem_Plugins\PluginAssemblies for full code.

We also need to register an Update plugin on the Bill entity so that we are able to get the correct total on the invoice when the bill items are added to the bill.

Follow the same steps to create an Update plugin on the Bill entity and fill in the information, as shown in the following screenshot. As we are writing an Update plugin, we need to register **Pre Image Alias** for our plugin, because in the case of the Update plugin, we will be able to get only the modified fields' value in the entity property bag. So if we want to get a field value even if it is not modified by the user, we need to register **Pre Image Alias**.

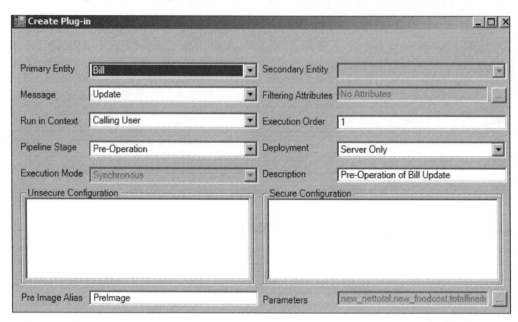

Double-click on `PreBillUpdate.cs` to open it in edit mode. In our Update plugin, instead of reading values from the entity property bag, we need to fetch the field's values from our `preImageentity` object. We can refer to an entity attribute in the same way that we refer to an entity object. Once we have calculated the value of the net total, we can inject that value into the entity property bag to store it in the CRM database.

```
protectedvoidExecutePreBillUpdate(LocalPluginContextlocalContext)
        {if (localContext == null){
thrownewArgumentNullException("localContext");}
IPluginExecutionContext context = localContext.PluginExecutionContext;
EntitypreImageEntity = (context.PreEntityImages !=
null&&context.PreEntityImages.Contains("PreImage")) ? context.
PreEntityImages["PreImage"] : null;
```

```
Entity entity = null;
if (context.InputParameters.Contains("Target") &&
context.InputParameters["Target"] isEntity)
            {
entity = (Entity)context.InputParameters["Target"];}
IOrganizationService service = localContext.OrganizationService;
Decimal _NetTotal = 0;
Decimal _FoodTotal = 0;
Decimal _RoomRent = 0;
Decimal _Percentage = 0;
Decimal _PercentageAmount = 0;
try
            {if (preImageEntity.Attributes.
Contains("totallineitemamount")){
_RoomRent = ((Money)preImageEntity.Attributes["totallineitemamount"]).
Value;}

if (preImageEntity.Attributes.Contains("new_foodcost"))
                {_FoodTotal = ((Money)preImageEntity.Attributes["new_
foodcost"]).Value;}
if (preImageEntity.Attributes.Contains("discountpercentage")){

_Percentage = ((Money)preImageEntity.Attributes["discountpercenta
ge"]).Value;}
_NetTotal = _FoodTotal + _RoomRent;
if (_Percentage > 0){
_PercentageAmount = (_NetTotal * _Percentage) / 100;
                _NetTotal = _NetTotal - _PercentageAmount;
                }

entity.Attributes.Add("new_nettotal", newMoney(_NetTotal));}
catch(Exception Ex)
            {thrownewInvalidPluginExecutionException(Ex.
InnerException.Message);}}
```

Now our plugin project is ready. Right-click on **Solution** to register all our plugins.

After registering the plugin, we should be able to see all of our plugins in **Plug-in Assemblies** in **CRM Explorer**. It should look like the following screenshot:

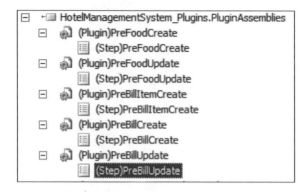

Now we can connect to our organization and test plugins.

Summary

In this chapter, we learned how we can leverage MS CRM 2011 to build a hotel management system. We learned how we can use sub-grids to show data from an associated view; we learned how we can set up a product catalog, and learned the basics of plugin development. We learned how we can write plugins using Developer Toolkit and deploy them in Microsoft CRM 2011. We also learned how to use images in plugins.

In the next chapter, we will see how we can use the Silverlight web resource in MS CRM 2011.

5
Using Web Resources in Microsoft CRM 2011

In this chapter we are going to discuss web resources. We will learn how we can create and associate web resources to Microsoft CRM 2011 entities. Web resources are a new feature added in Microsoft Dynamics 2011. We will learn about different types of web resources available in Microsoft CRM 2011 and how we can create Silverlight applications in Visual Studio 2010. We will also learn how we can deploy Silverlight web resources in Microsoft CRM 2011.

In this chapter we will cover the following topics:

- Understanding web resources in Microsoft CRM 2011
- Creating web resources in Microsoft CRM 2011
- Attaching a web resource to Microsoft CRM 2011 entities
- Creating a sample application using Bing Map Silverlight Control
- Introduction to Silverlight
- Introduction to Bing Maps
- Deploying the Silverlight application in Microsoft CRM 2011
- Introduction to dashboards in Microsoft CRM 2011
- Testing our application

Understanding web resources in Microsoft CRM 2011

Web resources in Microsoft CRM 2011 is a new feature; using a web resource we can share one resource with multiple entities. When we create a web resource, it is stored locally in the server and can be used in multiple entities. Web resources can be easily imported and exported from one environment to another within a solution. We can create different types of web resources as follows:

- Web page (HTML): We can create HTML web resources to create and embed a custom HTML page in entity forms

- Stylesheet (CSS):These web resources can be used to create a shared library of stylesheets, which can be used in other web resources

- Script (Jscript): We can use Script web resources to create reusable code libraries

- Data (XML): We can use XML web resources to store data in XML format; for example, if we need to store some configuration information, we can use XML web resources and can read them using client-side or server-side code

- PNG format: We can use this type of web resource to store PNG-format images

- JPG format: We can use this type of web resource to store JPG-format images

- GIF format: We can use this type of web resource to store GIF-format images

- Silverlight (XAP): We can use these web resources to upload Silverlight web resources, and can use them to enhance Microsoft CRM 2011 UI capability

- Stylesheet (XSL): We can use this type of web resource in XML and HTML web resources to apply XSL stylesheets

- ICO format: This type of web resource can be used to upload ICO-format images

Web resources can be accessed in different ways. When referring to a web resource using a site map or a ribbon button we can use a $webresource directive. Let's say we have one script web resource with a function OpenWeb and we want to refer that web resource within a ribbon button. We can refer to it using the following code snippet:

```
<Actions>
<JavaScriptFunctionFunctionName="OpenWeb"Library="
$webresource:new_mydemo.js" />
</Actions>
```

We can also reference web resources using relative and full URLs.

The relative URL is as follows:

```
<SCRIPT type=text/jscriptsrc="../new_/json2.js"></SCRIPT>
```

The full URL is as follows:

```
http://MSCRMSserver/Orrganization/WebResources/new_/json2.js
```

 When using a full URL in HTML or JavaScript web resources, we should always use `context.getServerUrl()` to get the correct server URL.

Creating web resources in Microsoft CRM 2011

We are going to use Microsoft CRM 2011 on-premise deployment for this application. In order to create a web resource, let's first create a solution. Open Microsoft CRM 2011 and create a solution named `MyDevelopment`.

 Please refer to *Chapter 2, Customizing Microsoft Dynamics CRM 2011*, on how to create solutions.

Use the following steps to create a web resource:

1. Navigate to **Setting| Solution** and open the **MyDevelopment** solution.
2. Navigate to **Web Resources** and click on **New.**

3. Enter a name in the **Name field** for the web resource.

4. Enter a name in the **Display Name field** for the web resource.

5. Select a type in the **Type field** for the web resource.

6. Select a language from the **Language field** for the web resource.

7. Save the web resource and then close.

Attaching a web resource to Microsoft CRM 2011 entities

Now we have a basic understanding of web resources, let's create a web resource of the type JavaScript that will have the function name `Hello`, and attach it to a Microsoft CRM 2011 entity.

Use the following steps to create a "Hello World" JavaScript web resource:

1. Navigate to **Settings | Solutions** and open the **MyDevelopment** solution.

2. Navigate to **Web Resources** and click on **New.**

3. Enter the following information:
    - **Name:** HelloWorld.js
    - **Display Name:** HelloWorld
    - **Type:** Script (Jscript)
    - **Language:** English

4. Click on **Text Editor.**

5. Enter the following code under **Source Field:**

```
function Hello()
{
alert('Welcome to Web Resource');
}
```

6. **Save** and **publish** the web resource.

Now that our web resource is ready, we can attach this web resource to the entity form and associate our `Hello` function with the form entity event. Let's call this function in the `OnLoad` event of the account entity form.

First we need to add the account entity to our solution. Once the account entity is added, use the following steps to attach our web resource with the entity form:

1. Navigate to **Entities | Account | Form.**

2. Open the **Account entity form.**

3. Click on the **Form Properties** ribbon button on the **Home** tab; the following screen will get displayed:

4. Click on the **Add** button to add a web resource to the entity form.

5. Browse in our list of web resources and add the one needed to the form.

6. Navigate to the **Event Handlers** section.

7. Click on the **Add** button to attach our web resource function to `OnLoad`, as seen in the following screenshot:

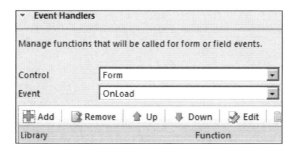

8. Select our **web resource** from our library's drop-down button.

9. Write our function name in the function text box, as shown in the following screenshot:

10. Click on **OK** to close the **Event Handlers** property window.

11. Click on **OK** to close the form property window.

12. **Save** and **close** the **Account** entity form.

13. **Publish** the account entity form.

Now, when we try creating a new account record, we should get a welcome pop up as shown in the following screenshot:

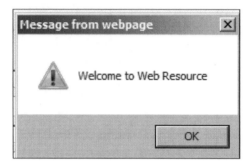

We can access Microsoft CRM 2011 data in JavaScript and Silverlight web resources. Microsoft CRM 2011 provides the following two endpoints for this:

- REST endpoint
- SOAP endpoint

REST endpoint

REST stands for **Representational State Transfer**. It works in a similar way to the Internet; for example, we can access resources on the Internet by their unique URIs, and in a similar way, in **REST** we can access every resource by its unique **URI**. We can write both synchronous and asynchronous requests using REST endpoints. Microsoft CRM 2011 provides a **Windows Communication Foundation (WCF)** data services framework to provide OData endpoints, which is a **REST**-based data service and is called Organization Data Service. In Microsoft CRM 2011, we can access Organization Data Service by using the **URI** [Your Organization Root URL]/xrmservices/2011/organizationdata.svc.

We can only `write`, `create`, `update`, `retrieve`, `delete`, `associate`, and `disassociate` requests using REST endpoints. You can refer to `http://msdn.microsoft.com/en-us/library/gg309549.aspx`for sample code to use **REST** endpoints in JavaScript and jQuery web resources.

SOAP endpoint

Microsoft CRM 2011 also provides SOAP endpoints, which provide access to all the methods on the Organization service. It does not support strong type; only the types defined in WSDL will be returned. You can refer to `http://msdn.microsoft.com/en-us/library/gg594434.aspx` to use SOAP endpoints in JavaScript.

 You can use an SOAP logger application that comes in Microsoft CRM 2011 SDK to generate client-side SOAP request. You can find this application under the `sdk\samplecode\cs\client\soaplogger` folder in SDK.

In both endpoints, the user is authenticated by the Microsoft CRM 2011 application itself, but we cannot use these endpoints outside of the Microsoft CRM 2011 application context.

Sample application using a Silverlight web resource

Let's create our sample application using Silverlight. We will create a Silverlight web resource using Bing Map Silverlight SDK, to show all accounts related to the current CRM user. We will display a pushpin for the account. Once our sample application is ready, we will upload this web resource on a dashboard in Microsoft CRM 2011. Before creating our application, we need to customize the account entity form and need to add the OOB **Latitude** and **Longitude** fields in the account entity form, as shown in the following screenshot:

We need to make sure we fill the **Latitude** and **Longitude** fields for our account to see pushpins for these accounts.

A Silverlight web resource

Silverlight is a powerful tool we can use to develop rich cross-browser applications. Silverlight supports most of the popular browsers and it can run on different devices as well. Microsoft CRM 2011 provides OOB support for Silverlight web resources. We can develop a Silverlight web application in Visual Studio having Silverlight tools installed and can deploy it as a Silverlight web resource in Microsoft CRM 2011. We also need to install Silverlight developer runtime if we want to debug our Silverlight application.

 You can download Silverlight runtime from `http://www.silverlight.net/downloads`.

Bing Maps basics

Bing Maps provides us a different set of tools that we can use to create a map application. We have options to use Bing Maps Ajax Control, Rest API, and Bing Maps Silverlight Control, to create a rich map application. Bing Maps also provides a tool for mobile application development. We can select a Bing Maps tool based on our application type. To develop a Bing Maps application, we need to create a developer account first. After creating a developer account, we need to register our application, where we will use the Bing Maps developer key.

 Please refer to `http://www.bingmapsportal.com/` to create a Bing Maps developer account.

Creating a sample application in Silverlight

Now let's create our sample application in Silverlight. To develop Silverlight applications we need to install the following tools first:

- Microsoft Silverlight 4 Tools for Visual Studio 2010
- Silverlight_Developer Runtime
- Bing Maps Silverlight Control SDK v1.0.1

You can download Bing Maps Silverlight Control SDK from `http://www.microsoft.com/en-in/download/details.aspx?id=2949`.

Once we have installed the tools mentioned, we can start our development. Use the following tools to create a Silverlight application in Visual Studio 2010:

1. Open Visual Studio 2010.
2. Select **File** from the main menu.
3. Select **New**, and then **Project** from the menu.
4. In the **New Project** dialog box, select **Silverlight**.
5. Select **Silverlight Application** from the available templates and then click on **OK**.

After carrying out these steps, we will see the following screen:

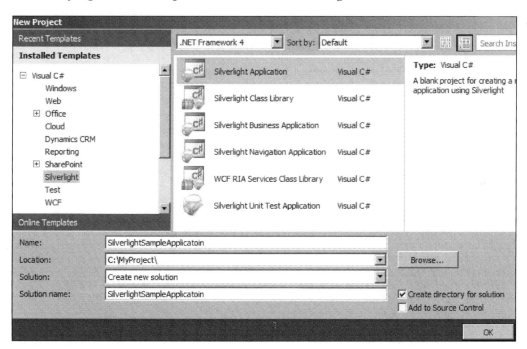

We will get another dialog box to host our Silverlight application; it will contain information about the web project name and its type. We can select the **Silverlight Version** option here. Please keep this as the default setting. This dialog box is as shown in the following screenshot:

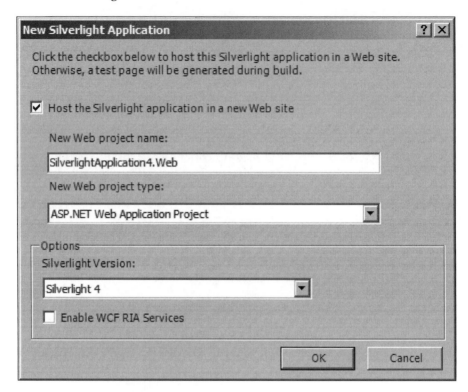

Adding a reference to Bing Maps Silverlight SDK

Once our application is created, we need to add a reference to the Silverlight SDK. Use the following steps to add a reference; make sure you have installed Silverlight Control SDK:

1. Right-click on the **Reference folder** and select **Add Reference**.
2. Browse to `c:\Programe Files (x86)\ Bing Maps Silverlight Control\V1\Libraries`.

3. Select both the libraries to add our Silverlight application as shown in the following screenshot:

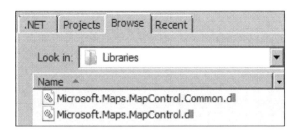

In our application, we are going to use the SOAP endpoint to connect Microsoft CRM 2011. We are now going to use the `SilverCrmSoap` library, which will have a built-in function that we can use to query the Microsoft CRM 2011 database. We need to add a reference of this library to our Silverlight application. This library can be downloaded from CodePlex.

Please download `SilverCrmSoap` from `http://silvercrmsoap.codeplex.com/`.

Now let's create classes for our application. Let's first design our class to hold our account information; we need to store the basic account information such as account name, account number, and address. We will be using this basic information to show under the tooltip when the user will move the mouse over the pushpins. We need to fetch the account's basic information to display in the tooltip with the account's latitude and longitude to draw pushpins.

Use the following steps to create an accounts class:

1. Right-click on our application in **Solution Explorer**.
2. Go to **Add | New Folder** and name it `Model`.
3. Right-click on the `Model` folder and go to **Add | New Item**.
4. Name it `Accounts.cs`.
5. Once we have added the `Accounts.cs` class, we need to add properties and methods to store the account information. You can find the code for the `Accounts.cs` file under `Chapter5\Code\SilverlightSampleApplication\ SilverlightSampleApplication\Model`.

After adding a class to hold the account information, we need a class to connect with the Microsoft CRM 2011 application. We need to write methods to authenticate the current user; for this we can use the existing silverlightutility.cs file. This class contains all the methods that we require, such as the function to get the SOAP server URL, the function to get the Microsoft CRM 2011 server URL and the function to get the Microsoft CRM 2011 context information. This class can be found at sdk\samplecode\cs\silverlight\soapforsilverlight\ soapforsilverlightsample. We can add this class to our Silverlight application. You can find this class under Chapter5\Code\SilverlightSampleApplication\ SilverlightSampleApplication\Model.

Now we need to create a class where we need to write functions to get the current CRM user and to get all accounts related to the current CRM user. So let's add a new class to our application and name it CrmUtility.cs. This class will contain methods to fetch data from Microsoft CRM.

This first method we will write in this class is to get the current user ID. We can use the WhoAMI class here. We will create an object of the OrganizationRequest class, which is a base class for all organization web service requests. We can pass an instance of a request class to the Execute method. Our method should look like the following code snippet:

```
publicvoidGetCurrentUserID()
{
try
{
this._d.BeginInvoke(delegate()
{
OrganizationRequestrequest = newOrganizationRequest()
{
RequestName = "WhoAmI"
};
IOrganizationService service =
SilverlightUtility.GetSoapService();
service.BeginExecute(request, newAsyncCallback(GetCurrentUserID_
Callback), service);
});
}
catch (Exception Ex)
{
throw Ex;
}

}
```

```
privatevoidGetCurrentUserID_Callback(IAsyncResult result)
{
try
{
this._d.BeginInvoke(delegate()
{
OrganizationResponse response = ((IOrganizationService)result.
AsyncState).EndExecute(result);
_currentUserID = (Guid)response["UserId"];
this.Count = this.Count - 1;
});

}
catch (Exception ex)
{
throw ex;
}
}
```

In the preceding record, we are checking for a response from the query and setting the Count flag that we used to trigger the property change event. Once we have the current user ID, we can fetch all accounts related to the current user. We can query the account entity and compare the owner ID with the current user ID. We also need to check the account state so that we can only fetch active accounts to be shown on the dashboard. Our function should look like the following code snippet:

```
publicvoidGetCurrentUserAccounts()
{
QueryExpressionquery = null;
string[] _AccountColumnToFetch= newstring[]
{
"name", "accountid", "accountnumber", "address1_latitude",
"address1_longitude", "address1_postalcode", "address1_city",
"address1_stateorprovince"
};

query = newQueryExpression()
{
EntityName = "account",
ColumnSet = newColumnSet()
{
Columns =
newObservableCollection<string>(_AccountColumnToFetch)
},
```

```
Criteria = newFilterExpression
{
FilterOperator = LogicalOperator.And,
Conditions ={newConditionExpression
{
AttributeName =   "address1_latitude",
    Operator = ConditionOperator.NotNull
},
newConditionExpression
{
AttributeName = "address1_longitude",
Operator = ConditionOperator.NotNull
},
newConditionExpression()
{
AttributeName = "statecode",
Operator = ConditionOperator.Equal,
Values = { 0 } // State = Active
},
newConditionExpression()
{
AttributeName = "ownerid",
Operator = ConditionOperator.Equal,
Values ={
this._currentUserID
}
 },
}
},
};
query.PageInfo = newPagingInfo
{
Count = MaxRecordsToReturn, PageNumber = 1, PagingCookie = null };
OrganizationRequest request = newOrganizationRequest()
{
RequestName = "RetrieveMultiple"
};
request["Query"] = query;
IOrganizationService service = SilverlightUtility.GetSoapService();
service.BeginExecute(request,
newAsyncCallback(RetrieveNearestRecords_Callback), service);

}
```

In the preceding code, we have used the `PageInfo` class to set the page properties that will help us deal with a large dataset. We have used the following properties for the `PageInfo` class:

- `Count`: This property is used to fetch the number of records
- `PageNumber`: This property is used to set which page we want to process first
- `PagingCookie`: This property is used to increase the performance of the application in the case of large datasets

We need to handle the callback for the `GetCurrentUserAccounts` function. You can find the full code under `Chapter5\Code\SilverlightSampleApplication\SilverlightSampleApplication\Model\CrmUtility.cs`.

Once we have the accounts, we need a function to show the pushpins for the collected accounts. We need to create an object of the `Pushpin` class, and then we can add the account's latitude and longitude, to show them in the Bing Map. Our function should look like the following code snippet:

```
publicvoidShowAccountSearchPushpins()
{
try{
{
MapLayer _CurrentAccountlayer =
(MapLayer)this._map.FindName("layerAccounts");
_CurrentAccountlayer.Children.Clear();
for (inti = 0; i<this._accounts.Count; i++)
{
    Pushpin _pushpinCurrentAcc = newPushpin();
_pushpinCurrentAcc.Name =
this._accounts[i].AccountID.ToString();
Location _LocationCurrentAcc = newLocation()
{
    Latitude = this._accounts[i].Latitude,
Longitude = this._accounts[i].Longitude
};
_pushpinCurrentAcc.Location = _LocationCurrentAcc;
StringBuilder _accountInfoprimary =
newStringBuilder();
                        _accountInfoprimary.Append("Account Number :"
+ this._accounts[i].ANumber + "\n");
                        _accountInfoprimary.Append("Account Name :" +
this._accounts[i].AName + "\n");
ToolTiptt =
AddToolTip(_accountInfoprimary.ToString());
```

```
ToolTipService.SetToolTip(_pushpinCurrentAcc,
tt);
this._map.Children.Add(_pushpinCurrentAcc);
}
}
catch (Exception ex)
        {
    throw ex;
    }
}
```

We have added all the required classes to our application. Now let's add a page to show the current CRM user accounts in Bing Map. Add a new folder called View, which will contain the main screen to show the account pushpins. Use the following steps to add a Silverlight page to the View folder:

1. Right-click on the View folder and go to **Add | New Item**.

2. Select **Silverlight Page** and name it MyAccounts.xaml as shown in the following screenshot:

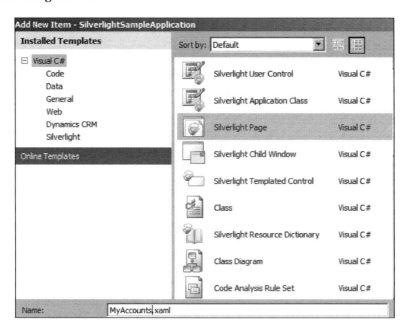

Now that we have added our Silverlight page, let's add a Map Control function in our **Account** page. Double-click on MyAccounts.xaml. We need to edit our user control file to add our Map Control function. After editing the user control file, our code should look like the following code snippet:

```
navigation:Pagex:Class="SilverlightSampleApplication.View.MyAccounts"
xmlns="http://schemas.microsoft.com/winfx/2006/xaml/
presentation"xmlns:x="http://schemas.microsoft.com/winfx/2006/xaml"
xmlns:d="http://schemas.microsoft.com/expression/blend/2008"
xmlns:mc="http://schemas.openxmlformats.org/markup-compatibility/2006"
mc:Ignorable="d"
xmlns:m="clr-namespace:Microsoft.Maps.MapControl;assembly=Microsoft.
Maps.MapControl"
xmlns:navigation="clr-namespace:System.Windows.
Controls;assembly=System.Windows.Controls.Navigation"
d:DesignWidth="640"d:DesignHeight="480" Title="MyAccounts Page">
<Grid x:Name="LayoutRoot">
<m:Map Name="MyMap"CredentialsProvider="Our Bing Maps Key"
Loaded="MyMap_Loaded">
<m:MapLayer x:Name="layerAccounts"></m:MapLayer></m:Map></Grid></
navigation:Page>
```

After modifying user control, if we will try to view our user control, it should look like the following screenshot:

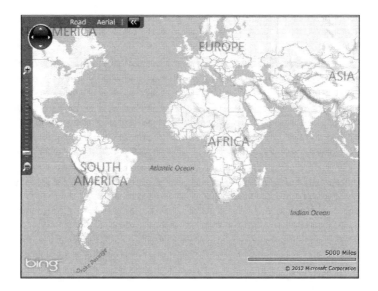

When we create our Silverlight application, we get a default Silverlight page with the **App.xaml** and **MainPage.xaml** files, as shown in the following screenshot:

We can use the App.xaml file to store the global resources for our application. We are going to store our crmutility object in the App.xaml.cs file. Open the App.xaml.cs file to edit and declare a public crmutlity class object, as follows:

```
public partial class App : Application
    {
publicCrmUtility _crmutility = new CrmUtility();
public App()
        {
this.Startup += this.Application_Startup;
this.Exit += this.Application_Exit;
this.UnhandledException +=
this.Application_UnhandledException;
        }
InitializeComponent();
}
```

Now let's edit our MainPage.xaml page; we will use this page to display a message to the CRM user till our application loads the account related to the current CRM user. We need to add a Frame and a TextBlock entity in our MainPage.xaml page. Open the MainPage.xaml file and edit the user control XAML file as shown in the following code snippet:

```
<UserControlx:Class="SilverlightSampleApplication.MainPage"
 xmlns="http://schemas.microsoft.com/winfx/2006/xaml/presentation"
xmlns:x="http://schemas.microsoft.com/winfx/2006/xaml"
xmlns:d="http://schemas.microsoft.com/expression/blend/2008"
 xmlns:mc="http://schemas.openxmlformats.org/markup-
compatibility/2006"
mc:Ignorable="d" Loaded="MyMap_Loaded"
d:DesignHeight="300"d:DesignWidth="400" xmlns:sdk="http://schemas.
microsoft.com/winfx/2006/xaml/presentation/sdk">
<Grid x:Name="LayoutRoot" Background="White">
<Grid.RowDefinitions>
<RowDefinition Height="*" />
<RowDefinition Height="Auto" />
<RowDefinition Height="Auto" />
<RowDefinition Height="*" />
</Grid.RowDefinitions>
<TextBlockx:Name="WaitMessage" Visibility="Visible" Text="Please wait
while we load your Accounts..."FontSize="24"Grid.Row="1"HorizontalAlig
nment="Center" Margin="10" />
<sdk:Frame Name="Frm" Visibility="Visible"Grid.Row="0"Grid.
RowSpan="4"/>
</Grid>
</UserControl>
```

In `MainPage.xaml.cs` we need to create an object of our `crmutility` class; first we will get the currently logged in CRM user. Once we have that user, we will fetch all accounts related to that user and show the account pushpins in the Silverlight page.

```
namespaceSilverlightSampleApplication
{
publicpartialclassMainPage : UserControl
    {
Appapp = (App)Application.Current;
CrmUtility _crmUtility;
publicMainPage()
        {
InitializeComponent();
_crmUtility = newCrmUtility(this.Dispatcher);
app._crmutility = this._crmUtility;
_crmUtility.PropertyChanged += (s, e) =>
{
if (e.PropertyName == "Ready")
{
this.WaitMessage.Visibility = Visibility.Collapsed;
this.Frm.Navigate(newUri("/View/MyAccounts.xaml",
UriKind.Relative));
}
};
}
privatevoidMyMap_Loaded(object sender, RoutedEventArgs e)
{
_crmUtility.GetCurrentUserID();
}
}
}
```

Deploying the Silverlight application in Microsoft CRM 2011

Now our application is ready, let's deploy it in Microsoft CRM 2011. Use the following steps to deploy the Silverlight web resource in Microsoft CRM 2011:

1. Right-click on **SilverlightSampleApplication** and select **Build**.
2. Open Microsoft CRM 2011 and navigate to our **MyDevelopment** solution.

3. Navigate to **Web Resources** and click on **New** to create a new web resource.

4. Fill in the following properties:
   ° **Name:** /SilverightSampleApplication.Xap
   ° **Display Name:** SilverlightSampleApplication
   ° **Type:** Silverlight (XAP)
   ° **Language:** English
   ° **Upload File :** Browse SilverlightSampleApplication.xap file.

 You should get the SilverlightSampleApplication.
xap file under SilverlightSampleApplication\
SilverlightSampleApplication.Web\ClientBin.

5. **Save** and **publish** the web resource.

After publishing our web resource, it should look like the following screenshot:

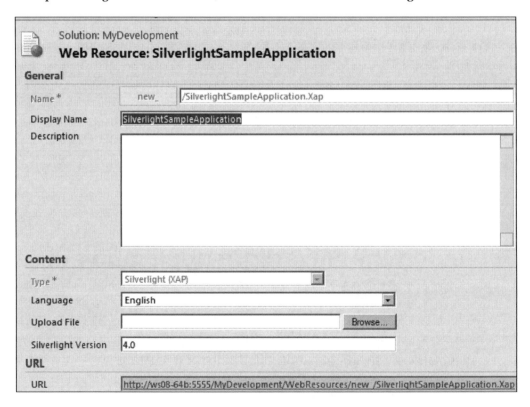

Introduction to dashboards in Microsoft CRM 2011

Dashboards are a new feature added in Microsoft CRM 2011, which help us to easily access all of our business data in different formats. We can use different components such as charts, graph, lists, IFrame, web page, and Silverlight web resources in a dashboard to view Microsoft CRM 2011 data. By default, a single dashboard can have six components. We can easily create dashboards using the OOB templates available in Microsoft CRM 2011.

 In the Microsoft CRM 2011 on-premise deployment, we can use PowerShell to increase the number of components to be displayed on a dashboard.

Now let's create a dashboard in Microsoft CRM 2011 to host our Silverlight web resource. Use the following steps to create the dashboard and place our web resource in it:

1. Navigate to **Dashboards** from the left-hand side navigation section and select **New**:

2. Select **Dashboard Layout** and click on **Create**.

3. Name it Show Accounts.

4. Remove all web resource containers except one.

5. Click on the **Insert Web Resource** button as shown in the following screenshot:

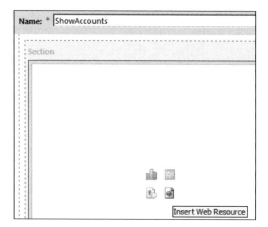

6. Browse to our Silverlight web resource and name it `showaccounts` as shown in the following screenshot:

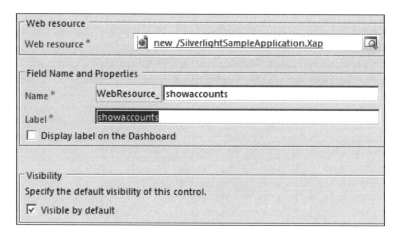

7. Adjust the web resource layout accordingly.

8. Click on Save and Close.

Testing our application

Once our dashboard is created, we can test our application. We need to make sure all accounts have latitude and longitude values filled in the respective latitude and longitude fields in the account entity. For our sample application, we have used sample account data and found latitude and longitude based on their zip codes.

When we will try to browse our dashboard, we will get the following screen initially:

Please wait while we load your Accounts...

And once it fetches all accounts related to the current CRM user, we should see all the account pushpins related to us, as shown in the following screenshot:

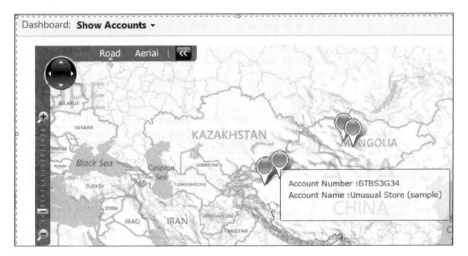

Summary

In this chapter we learned about the web resource feature in Microsoft CRM 2011 and their types. We learned how we can reference web resources in Microsoft CRM 2011 entity forms, how we can create Silverlight applications, and how to deploy them in Microsoft CRM 2011. We also learned how we can place a Silverlight web resource on a dashboard.

In the next chapter we are going to see how we can deploy a custom web application in Microsoft CRM 2011.

6
Using External Web Applications in Microsoft CRM 2011

In this chapter we are going to use Microsoft CRM 2011 web services to create a custom web application. We will learn different ways of accessing Microsoft CRM 2011 data in web applications. We will learn how to create entity records from a custom web application. We will also learn how to create an editable grid for an associated entity.

We will cover the following topics in this chapter:

- Application development for Microsoft CRM 2011
- Early bound classes
- Late bound classes
- Microsoft CRM 2011 web services
- Creating editable grid views for Microsoft CRM 2011
- Deploying custom web applications to Microsoft CRM 2011
- The testing application

Application development for Microsoft CRM 2011

Microsoft CRM 2011 provides a rich API and web service support to enhance its capabilities. We can develop a rich application using different methods for Microsoft CRM 2011. We have the following options to use:

- Early bound classes
- Late bound classes
- Using REST
- Using SOAP

We can develop a custom web application or Silverlight application to create, edit, or display Microsoft CRM 2011 data. We can also develop an HTML web resource to manipulate Microsoft CRM 2011 data.

If you want to develop a custom portal to expose Microsoft CRM 2011 data, we have the option of using existing portal accelerators or we can develop our own custom portal.

> You can check Microsoft Pinpoint (`http://dynamics.pinpoint.microsoft.com/en-US/home`) for the latest portal released for Microsoft CRM 2011.

Microsoft CRM SDK comes with rich documentation and with portal development tools that we can use to create a tightly integrated application with Microsoft CRM 2011.

> Note that if you want to develop a portal to expose Microsoft CRM data to non-CRM users, we need to consider an external user license. If you are a Microsoft partner, you can refer to license information in PartnerSource.

Early bound classes

If you want to enjoy intelliSense support during development, you can use early bound classes. Microsoft CRM 2011 provides us with the ability to generate a class from its metadata, which includes all OOB and custom entity customization. Microsoft CRM SDK comes with a utility, CrmSvcUtil, that can be used to generate early bound classes. It creates a class file that includes strongly typed classes for all Microsoft CRM entities. This tool creates one class for each entity and provides intelliSense support during development.

You can refer to the following syntaxes to generate early bound classes depending on your deployment.

On-premise deployment

For on-premise deployment, use the following syntax:

```
CrmSvcUtil.exe /url:http://<servername>/<organizationname>/
XRMServices/2011/Organization.svc
    /out:<outputfilename>.cs /username:<username> /password:<password>
/domain:<domainname>
    /namespace:<outputnamespace> /serviceContextName:<service context
name>
```

Online deployment

If you are using online deployment, you can use the following syntax:

```
CrmSvcUtil.exe
/url:https://myorg.crm.dynamics.com/XRMServices/2011/Organization.svc
/out:GeneratedCode.cs /username:username@live.com
/password:yourpassword!
```

IFD deployment

If you are using IFD deployment, you need to use the following syntax:

```
CrmSvcUtil.exe
/url:https://myorg.crm.com:555/XRMServices/2011/Organization.svc
/out:GeneratedCode.cs /username:administrator /password:yourpassword
```

You can refer to http://msdn.microsoft.com/en-us/library/gg327844.aspx for more details on the CrmSvcUtil utility.

Once an early bound class is generated, it can be added in our application to connect to our organization. We can refer to our OOB entity and custom entity directly in our code. Early bound classes basically provide compile-time checking for all entity and attribute types. The following code snippet is an example of creating a contact record using an early bound class:

```
Contact contact = new Contact(){
    FirstName = "Mahender",
    LastName = "Pal",
    Address1_StateOrProvince = "Haryana",
    Address1_PostalCode = "131001",};
Guid _contactId = _serviceProxy.Create(contact);
```

An early bound class provides intelliSense support and compile-time validation, which help us to decrease our development time, but it also adds overhead to generate early bound classes every time we make any customization changes.

Late bound classes

In the late bound programming method, we use the Entity class to refer to OOB and custom entities. Using late bound classes, we can refer to entities and attributes that may not exist during compile time. The late bound class method performs type checking at runtime. While using a late bound class, we will not get any type of intelliSense support, so we need to make sure to reference the correct field entity and attribute names. In the late bound method we use logical attribute names instead of schema names. The following code snippet is an example of creating a contact using a late bound class:

```
Entity _Contact=new Entity("contact");
_Contact["firstname"]="Mahender";
_Contact["lastname"]="Pal";
Guid _ContactId=_service.Create(_Contact);
```

Late bound classes help us to write code for those entities that are not yet created and they also use fewer resources as compared to early bound classes. But, they do not provide any intelliSense support, so we need to know the exact logical name of the entity and attributes.

Microsoft CRM 2011 web services

Microsoft CRM 2011 provides rich WCF service support. Microsoft CRM 2011 provides the two following web services.

Organization web service

The Organizaiton web service is used to retrieve data and metadata from Microsoft CRM 2011. It has the following methods.

Create

The Create method is used to create entity records. It takes the entity object as a parameter and returns the GUID of the newly created record. We can use the following example to create the Account entity record:

```
Entity Account = new Entity("account");
Account.Attributes.Add("name", "TestAccount");
Account.Attributes.Add("address1_city","Gurgaon");
service.Create(Account);
```

Update

The Update method is used to update existing entity data based on key values. It takes the entity object as a parameter. For example, if we want to update city information for a particular account, we can write the following function:

```
private void UpdateAccount(IOrganizationService service,Guid
AccountID)
    {
        Entity Account = new Entity("account");
        Account["address1_city"] = "CA";
        Account["accountid"] = AccountID;
        service.Update(Account);
    }
```

Delete

This method is used to delete entity records. It takes the entity name and GUID of the record that we want to delete. The following code snippet is an example of the Delete method:

```
service.Delete("account", AccountID);
```

Retrieve

The `Retrieve` method is used to retrieve data from CRM entities based on the key value. It takes the entity name, the GUID of the record, and the column that we want to fetch. For example, we can use the following code to fetch account records:

```
Entity _Account = service.Retrieve("account",AccountID, new
ColumnSet(new string[] { "name", "accountcategorycode"})));
```

RetrieveMultiple

The `RetrieveMultiple` method is used to fetch data from CRM entities based on the condition available in the query object passed to this method. This method returns entity collection.

```
QueryExpression _Query = new QueryExpression("account");
        ColumnSet _Cols = new ColumnSet(new string[] { "name",
"accountcategorycode", "parentaccountid" });
        ConditionExpression _Condition = new ConditionExpression();
        _Condition.AttributeName = "address1_city";
        _Condition.Operator = ConditionOperator.Equal;
        _Condition.Values.Add("CA");
        _Query.ColumnSet = _Cols;
        _Query.Criteria.AddCondition(_Condition);
        EntityCollection Entity = service.RetrieveMultiple(_Query);
```

Execute

The `Execute` method can be used to perform those operations that are not exposed as methods in the CRM service. It takes `Request` as a parameter and returns `Response` as output. For example, we can use the following request to assign an account to a Microsoft CRM 2011 user and pass the account to the `Execute` method:

```
AssignRequest Request = new AssignRequest
            {
              Assignee = new EntityReference("systemuser", UserID),
                Target = new EntityReference("account", AccountID)
            };
AssignResponse Response = (AssignResponse)service.Execute(Request);
```

Associate

The `Associate` method is used create links between two entity records. For example, we can use the following code to relate account IDs to contacts:

```
//Create a collection of the entity ids that will be associated to the
contact.
        EntityReferenceCollection relatedEntities = new
EntityReferenceCollection();
        relatedEntities.Add(new EntityReference("account",
account1Id));
        relatedEntities.Add(new EntityReference("account",
account2Id));
        relatedEntities.Add(new EntityReference("account",
account3Id));
        Relationship relationship = new Relationship("account_primary_
contact");
        service.Associate("contact", contactId, relationship,
relatedEntities);
```

Disassociate

The `Disassociate` method is used to remove links between two entity records.
The following code snippet is an example of disassociating entity records associated
in the previous method:

```
        service.Disassociate("contact", _contactId, relationship,
relatedEntities);
```

In order to access metadata, we need to use metadata classes. You can refer to `http://technet.microsoft.com/en-us/library/gg307336.aspx` to get information on
metadata classes for Microsoft CRM 2011.

Discovery web service

DiscoveryService is used to get lists of organizations for a CRM user. This web service
only contains one method, the `Execute` method. The following code snippet is an
example of fetching all organization information:

```
RetrieveOrganizationsRequest orgsRequest =new
RetrieveOrganizationsRequest()
            { AccessType = EndpointAccessType.Default,
              Release = OrganizationRelease.Current
            };
        RetrieveOrganizationsResponse organizations =
RetrieveOrganizationsResponse)service.Execute(orgsRequest);
```

Creating editable grid views for Microsoft CRM 2011

We are going to use late bound classes for our sample application. We will create a custom ASP.NET website for our on-premise deployment. If you are reading chapters continually, you will be aware of the hotel management system application that we created in *Chapter 4, Implementing Business Logic through Plugins*. We are going to deploy our custom `asp.net` website for the same application. We will create an editable grid to keep food item details for the customer. We will place our editable grid in the Contact entity by using IFRAME. Hotel staff can use this application to add, delete, and update food item details.

So let's create our sample web application. Perform the following steps to create a web application:

1. Open Visual Studio 2010.
2. Select **New | Web Site...**.
3. Select **Visual C# | ASP.NET Empty Web Site**.
4. Name it `FooditemsDetails`.

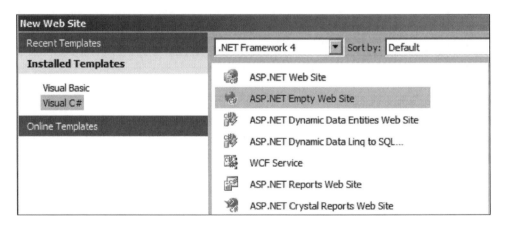

5. Right-click on the website and select **Add New Item**.
6. Select **Web Form** and name it `FoodItemDetails.aspx`.

Now we have our page ready, let's add a reference to Microsoft CRM 2011 SDK. Perform the following steps to add an SDK reference:

1. Right-click on the website and select **Add Reference**.
2. Browse to `microsoft.xrm.sdk.dll` to add to our website.

First, we need to add the class to connect to our organization. As we are using on-premise deployment and AD authentication, we need to pass user credentials to create the CRM service object. We can store this information in the `web.config` file, which can be changed if required during deployment of our web application.

 You can encrypt the username and password in the `web.config` file.

Right-click on our website, add a new class, and name it `crmutility.cs`. First, we need to get the Organization service object to query Microsoft CRM 2011 data. We can create an Organization service object as per the following code snippet:

```
private void CreateService()
    {//read user name from web.config file
string UserID = ConfigurationManager.AppSettings["UserID"];
        string ServiceURL = ConfigurationManager.AppSettings["Organiza
tionServiceURL"];
        string Password = ConfigurationManager.
AppSettings["Password"];
        string _DomainName = ConfigurationManager.
AppSettings["DomainName"];
        ClientCredentials Credentials = new ClientCredentials();
        Credentials.Windows.ClientCredential = new System.Net.Ne
tworkCredential(UserID,Password,_DomainName); CredentialCache.
DefaultNetworkCredentials;
        Uri OrganizationUri = new Uri(ServiceURL);
        using (OrganizationServiceProxy serviceProxy = new Organizatio
nServiceProxy(OrganizationUri, null, Credentials, null))
        {
    _iOgranizationService = (IOrganizationService)serviceProxy;
        }
    }
```

Now we need to write three main functions to create, update, and delete the Food Details entity record. We will see three fields in our grid view menu, which is an option set field that contains the cost and quantity of the food.

Let's write our `Add` function, which will add a new record to the Food entity. For this, we will use the `Create` method of the Organization service. Our function should look like the following code:

```
public void AddFoodItem(int _MenuValue,Decimal Cost,int Quantity,Guid
contactid)
```

```
    {
        Entity _Food = new Entity("new_food");
        _Food.Attributes["new_menu"] = new OptionSetValue(_MenuValue);
        _Food.Attributes["new_quantity"] = Quantity;
        _Food.Attributes["new_cost"] = new Money(Cost);
        _Food.Attributes["new_fooddetailsid"] = new
EntityReference("contact", contactid);
        _Food.Attributes["new_orderdate"] = DateTime.Now.
ToLocalTime();
        _iOgranizationService.Create(_Food);


    }
```

Microsoft CRM 2011 now uses native .NET types for most of the data types, so we used the **Money** field to typecast the **Currency** field. You can refer to `http://msdn.microsoft.com/en-us/library/gg328507.aspx` to get information about new Microsoft CRM 2011 data types. In the previous function, we also used the `DateTime.Now.ToLocalTime()` property to get the time in the local time format. Microsoft CRM 2011 will convert it automatically to the UTC format because Microsoft CRM 2011 stores all date fields in the database in the UTC format.

We also need a function to delete the selected record, so for deleting a record we can use the following code:

```
public void Delete(Guid _Foodid)
{_iOgranizationService.Delete("new_food", _Foodid); }
```

Now, let's write a function to fetch all food details for a particular contact. We will pass the current contact ID to our web application. We will use the same contact ID to fetch data from Microsoft CRM 2011 for the Food entity. Our function should look like the following code snippet:

```
public DataTable GetFoodItemsDetails(Guid ContactID)
    {  //First create data table
DataTable _Food = new DataTable();
        _Food.Columns.Add("Menu");
        _Food.Columns.Add("Cost");
        _Food.Columns.Add("Quantity");
        _Food.Columns.Add("ID");
    //build query to fetch data from Microsoft CRM 2011
        QueryExpression _Query = new QueryExpression
            {   EntityName = "new_food",
                ColumnSet = new ColumnSet("new_menu", "new_cost",
"new_quantity"),
```

```
                    Criteria =
                    {   FilterOperator = LogicalOperator.And,
                        Conditions =
                            { new ConditionExpression
    {   AttributeName="new_fooddetailsid",
                                Operator=ConditionOperator.Equal,
                                Values={ContactID}
                        } } }      };
 EntityCollection _Entities = _iOgranizationService.RetrieveMultiple(_
Query);
            foreach (Entity _Contact in _Entities.Entities)
            {   DataRow dr = _Food.NewRow();
                if (_Contact.Attributes.Contains("new_menu"))
                {dr["Menu"] = RetrieveOptionSetValue(((OptionSetVal
ue)_Contact.Attributes["new_menu"]).Value);}
                if (_Contact.Attributes.Contains("new_cost"))
                { dr["Cost"] = ((Money)_Contact.Attributes["new_
cost"]).Value;}
                if (_Contact.Attributes.Contains("new_quantity"))
                { dr["Quantity"] = _Contact.Attributes["new_
quantity"].ToString();}
                dr["ID"] = _Contact.Id;
                _Food.Rows.Add(dr);
            }
            return _Food; }
```

The last function that we need is used to update existing food details, and it should look like the following code snippet:

```
    public void UpdateFoodItem(int _MenuValue, Decimal Cost, int
Quantity, Guid contactid,Guid Foodid)
    {
        Entity _Food = new Entity("new_food");
        _Food.Attributes["new_foodid"] = Foodid;
        _Food.Attributes["new_menu"] = new OptionSetValue(_MenuValue);
        _Food.Attributes["new_quantity"] = Quantity;
        _Food.Attributes["new_cost"] = new Money(Cost);
        _Food.Attributes["new_fooddetailsid"] = new
EntityReference("contact", contactid);

        _iOgranizationService.Update(_Food);

    }
```

We have used the Update method of the Organization service. Based on the primary fields, we are updating the Food entity data.

Now, we have all the required functions, so let's design our editable grid view. Open the web form that we added to our website, go to design mode, and add a grid view control to our web page. We need to add a template field in our grid view. Perform the following steps to add a template column:

1. Click on the grid view task button and click on **Edit Column**.
2. Add four template fields, as shown in the following screenshot:

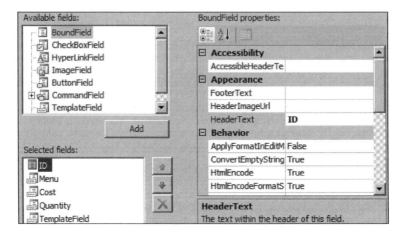

We will be using the **ID** field to hold the Food entity record GUID. Once **TemplateField** is added, let's modify the template column to add required controls.

Click on the grid view task button and select **Edit Template**.

We need to add controls in the edit template, as shown in the following screenshot:

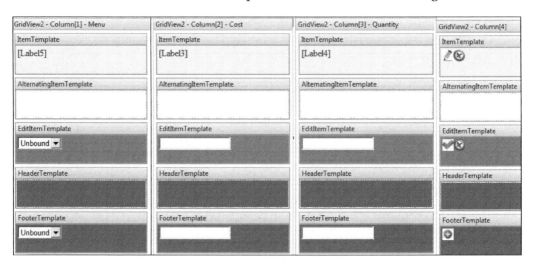

We can also apply **Auto Format** from the grid view task button. After making these changes, our grid view should look like the following screenshot:

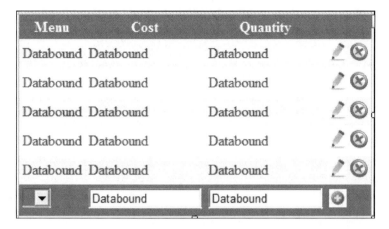

First, we need to write a function to bind data to our grid view. We need to get all Food entity data based on the contact ID and the bind result set to our grid view. Our data bind function should like the following code snippet:

```
private void DataBind()
    {    DataTable dt = _object.GetFoodItemsDetails(contactid);
        if (dt.Rows.Count > 0)
        {    GridView2.DataSource = dt;
            GridView2.DataBind();
        }
        else
        {
            dt.Rows.Add(dt.NewRow());
            GridView2.DataSource = dt;
            GridView2.DataBind();
            int columncount = GridView2.Rows[0].Cells.Count;
            GridView2.Rows[0].Cells.Clear();
            GridView2.Rows[0].Cells.Add(new TableCell());
            GridView2.Rows[0].Cells[0].ColumnSpan = columncount;
            GridView2.Rows[0].Cells[0].Text = "No Records Found";
        }
    }
```

Now we need to add an event to our grid view. Perform the following steps to add an event to the grid view:

1. Right-click on the grid view and select **Properties**.

2. Select the **Event** tab and double-click on the following event names one by one:

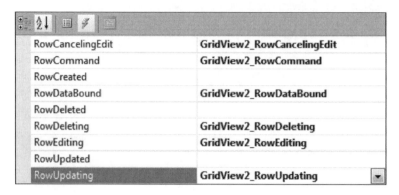

RowCancelingEdit	GridView2_RowCancelingEdit
RowCommand	GridView2_RowCommand
RowCreated	
RowDataBound	GridView2_RowDataBound
RowDeleted	
RowDeleting	GridView2_RowDeleting
RowEditing	GridView2_RowEditing
RowUpdated	
RowUpdating	GridView2_RowUpdating

Once these events are generated, we need to write code for them. You can get the full code from `Chapter6\Code\FooditemDetails` in the code bundle.

Deploying custom web applications to Microsoft CRM 2011

Now it's time to deploy our web application to Microsoft CRM 2011. In Microsoft CRM 4.0, we used to deploy custom web applications in the ISV folder, but in Microsoft CRM 2011, calling the Microsoft Dynamics CRM 2011 web services from the `<crmwebroot>\ISV` folder is no longer supported. The ISV folder has officially been deprecated, so any custom code or custom web page deployed in this folder must use only 2007 service endpoints. Let's create a virtual directory for our website under IIS. Perform the following steps to set the virtual directory:

1. Open Internet Information via **Control Panel | Administrative Task | Internet Information Services**.

2. Select **Server Name | Sites | Default Web Site**.

3. Right-click on **Default Web Site** and select **Add Application**.

4. Enter the following information:

    1. **Alias:** `FooditemDetails`

2. **Physical Path**: Select the location for your web project.

3. **Application Pool**: Keep it at the default value.

5. Click on **OK**.

Once configuration has been done, the website tree should like the following screenshot:

Now let's access our web application in Microsoft CRM 2011:

1. Open the `Development` solution that we created in *Chapter 4, Implementing Business Logic through Plugins*.

2. Navigate to **Web Resources**.

3. Click on **New** to create a new web resource.

4. Enter the following information in the web resource dialog box:

    1. **Name**: `contactWR.js`

    2. **Display Name**: `contact`

    3. **Type**: `Script (JavaScript)`

5. Open the text editor and enter the following code:

```
function ShowCustomWeb()
{
var ID=Xrm.Page.data.entity.getId();
var URL="http://localhost/FoodDetails/FooditemDetails.aspx?id="+ID
//get iframe
var IFRAME=Xrm.Page.getControl("IFRAME_fooddetail").setSrc(URL);

}
```

6. Click on **Save** and publish the web resource.

Now we have our web resource ready and need to attach this web resource to the Customer entity. We also need to add the IFRAME in the Customer entity form. Perform the following steps to customize the Customer entity:

1. Navigate to the **Customer** entity and open the Customer form to customize it.

2. Remove **Sub-Grid** from the **Food Details** section.

3. Navigate to the **Insert** tab from the form ribbon toolbar and select **IFRAME**:

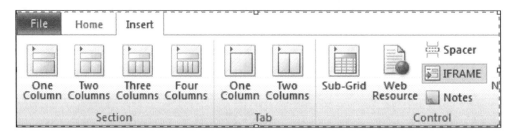

4. Enter the following information in the **IFRAME** tab:

    1. **Name:** IFRAME_fooddetail

    2. **URL:** #

5. Uncheck the **Restrict cross frame scripting** checkbox.

6. Click on **Form Properties** in our web resource.

7. Attach the **ShowCustomWeb** function to form the **OnLoad** event:

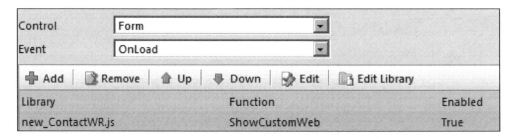

8. Click on **Save** to save the changes, and then click on **Publish** to publish the form.

The testing application

Now let's test our application. When we try to open any customer record, we should be able to see the Food entity record in the grid view, as in the following screenshot:

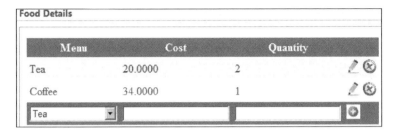

Now we can add, update, and delete the Food Detail entity record from our grid view.

Summary

In this chapter, we learned about application development for Microsoft CRM 2011, different methods of accessing Microsoft CRM 2011 data, and about web services available in Microsoft CRM 2011 and their methods. We also learned how to create an editable grid view and deploy it in Microsoft CRM 2011.

In the next chapter we will learn about the mobile client and different methods of accessing Microsoft CRM 2011 data on mobile devices.

7
Using Mobile Client in Microsoft CRM 2011

In this chapter we are going to learn about the mobile client for Microsoft CRM 2011. We will learn how to configure Mobile Express forms, and also the security roles required to access Microsoft CRM 2011 in mobile devices. We will also learn how to expose Microsoft CRM 2011 entities for mobile devices. We will see how we can create and modify an existing record in Mobile Express and discuss the mobile add-ons available in the market. In this chapter we are going to discuss the following topics:

- Introduction to the mobile client for Microsoft CRM 2011
- Security permissions required for Mobile Express
- Accessing Mobile Express
- Entities exposed to Mobile Express
- Functionality available in Mobile Express
- The Mobile Express form
- The Mobile Express view
- Creating and editing Microsoft CRM 2011 data
- Other mobile solutions for Microsoft CRM 2011

Introduction to the mobile client for Microsoft CRM 2011

Microsoft CRM has a new feature called **Mobile Express**; in Microsoft CRM 4.0 we need to install Mobile Express, but in Microsoft CRM 2011 it is a part of the default installation. This allows us to access Microsoft CRM 2011 through mobile devices. We can access Microsoft CRM 2011 using various mobile devices.

 You can download Mobile Express for Microsoft CRM 4.0 from `http://www.microsoft.com/en-us/download/details.aspx?id=20353`.

If your mobile device browser supports HTML 4.0, you can access Microsoft CRM 2011. The following table lists some of the supported devices that can be used to access Microsoft CRM 2011:

Mobile Device	Operating System	Supporting Browser
All Windows Phones	Windows Phone 7	Internet Explorer
HTC HD2	Windows Mobile 6.5	Internet Explorer and Opera
HTC Fuze, HTC Touch HD	Windows Mobile 6.5	Internet Explorer
Nokia N97 mini, Nokia E71, Nokia	Nokia S60, Nokia S40	Nokia
All Android	Android	All
iPhone 3, 4	iOS	Safari
BlackBerry Storm, Storm2, and Curve	BlackBerry OS	BlackBerry, Opera
Palm Pre	Palm WebOS	Palm
Sony Ericsson w8	Android	Android

Security permissions required for Mobile Express

Microsoft CRM 2011 users will be able to access entities if they have assigned a security role with the **Go Mobile** access privilege. We can set up the required permission for the security role provided to the user. Use the following steps to set up security for mobile access:

1. Navigate to **Settings** | **Administration** | **Security Roles**.

2. Open the security role assigned to the user.

3. Navigate to the **Business Management** tab.

4. Make sure **Go Mobile** has organizational access in **Miscellaneous Privileges**, as shown in the following screenshot:

Accessing Mobile Express

We can access Mobile Express from our browser; it is an easy way to test our Mobile Express customization. So instead of testing our customization on a mobile, we can simply access Mobile Express from our computer's browser by just appending /m in our organizational URL. We can access our on-premise deployment using `http://CRMServer/Organization/m`.

In the same way, if we are using online deployment, we can access using `https://orgnizationname.crm5.dynamics.com/m`, and it will look like the following screenshot:

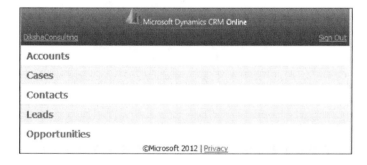

It will show the OOB Mobile Express enabled entities. Online deployment can be used on mobile devices through Internet connectivity.

But we are using on-premise deployment, which is available only in our intranet; we have the following options to access our Microsoft CRM 2011 environment:

- Configure IFD, so that Microsoft CRM 2011 users can access Mobile Express by connecting to the Internet

- Allow CRM users to connect to your network so that they can access the mobile using Internet connectivity

Entities exposed to Mobile Express

Almost all the system entities are available for Mobile Express. When we access Mobile Express, we will be able to see the default entities, as shown in the following screenshot, but we can configure other system entities for Mobile Express easily:

Let's say we want to enable Mobile Express for the **Quote** entity. Use the following steps for configuring Mobile Express in Microsoft CRM 2011 entities:

1. Navigate to your solution.

2. Navigate to **Components | Entities | Quote**.

3. Enable the **Mobile Express** checkbox under the **Outlook& Mobile** section, as shown in the following screenshot:

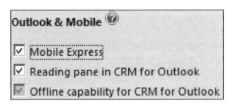

4. Click on **Save** and publish the entity.

Now when we try to access Mobile Express, we should be able to see the **Quote** entity with the other entities on the list, as seen in the following screenshot:

Functionalities available in Mobile Express

In Mobile Express, not all entities are available for creation or modification. We can access some entities directly and some entities are only available through related entities, as seen in the following screenshot:

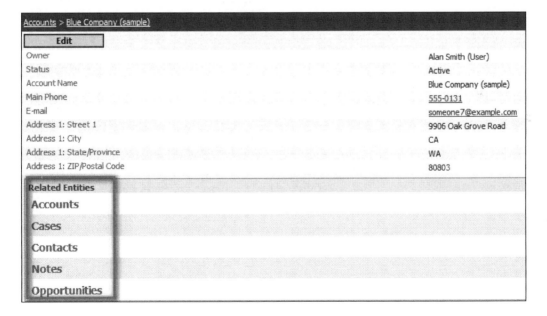

The following table provides functions for Microsoft CRM 2011 entities for Mobile Express:

Entity	Functionality Available
Account, Case, Contact, Lead, Note, Opportunity, Task, Custom Entity	Available for Create and Modify
Address, Appointment, Campaign, Campaign Activity, Campaign Response, Competitor, Contract, Contract Line, Discount, Discount List, Email, Fax, Invoice, Invoice Product, Letter, Marketing List, Opportunity Close , Opportunity Product, Order, Order Product, Phone call, Price List, Price List Item, Product, Quote, Quote Close, Quote Product, Service Activity, Subject, Unity, Unity Group, User	Available for View only

The Mobiles Express form

In Microsoft CRM 2011, every entity system or custom has two forms. The OOB **Main** form type is used when the Microsoft CRM 2011 application is accessed by a web client or outlook client and **Mobile** is used when the Microsoft CRM 2011 application is accessed by mobile devices, as shown in the following screenshot:

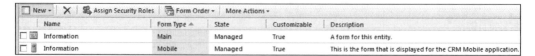

Microsoft CRM 2011 also has a new functionality to set up multiple forms, so we can create multiple mobiles or main forms. After that, we can control visibility of CRM forms using security roles. We can assign security roles for Microsoft CRM 2011 forms using the **Assign Security Roles** option. For example, if you have multiple sections that you want to hide from salespersons, you can create a form and remove those form sections and assign a **Sales Person** security role to that form, so this form will be visible to salespersons only.

Creating and customizing mobile forms

We can customize OOB mobile forms and can also create new mobile forms if required. We can select the attribute that we want to show Mobile Express. Let's say we want to create another mobile form for a contact entity.

Use the following rules to create new entities for a mobile device:

1. Navigate to your solution.
2. Go to **Components** | **Entities** | **Contact** | **Form**.
3. Select **Mobile Form** from the **New** drop-down menu as shown in the following screenshot:

4. We can add the required fields to the **Mobile Form** form we are creating.
5. Select **Form Properties** and give a name to your custom form.
6. Click on **Save and Close** and publish your entity.

These steps on the entity form are as shown in the following screenshot:

If we need to customize the existing mobile form, perform the following steps:

1. Navigate to your solution.
2. Go to **Components | Entities | Contact | Form**.
3. Select the mobile form that we want to customize.
4. Double-click on the form or go to **More Actions | Edit**.
5. Add the required fields and click on **Save and Close**.
6. Publish your entity.

> The attributes that are listed on the **Selected Attributes** side will be displayed on the mobile form in the order in which they are listed.

Microsoft CRM 2011 also provides us with the functionality to set up read only fields for the mobile form. We can select the field from the **Selected Attributes** section and click on the **Read Only** button to make that field read-only in mobile forms.

The Mobile Express view

Every CRM entity can have multiple system views and we can also create a custom view, if required, to implement our specific requirement. There is a default view for every entity that is presented to the user when any CRM entity is selected from the navigation area to the left. We can set the default view according to our requirement for our web client. But Mobile Express always uses the system default view to present the user list of the record for the CRM entity. So changing the default view won't change the default view for Mobile Express; it will still use the same default view for that entity, as shown in the following screenshot:

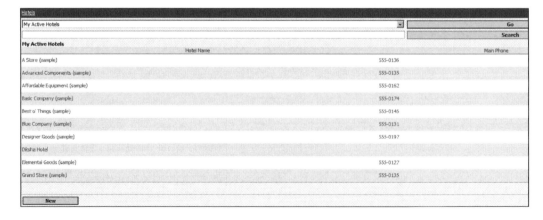

But we can access all the views available in Microsoft CRM 2011. We can select the view from the **View** drop down and select the **Go** button to open that view. We also search for the required records by typing a keyword in the search textbox available and clicking the **Search** button.

Creating and editing Microsoft CRM 2011 data

We can create and edit the Microsoft CRM 2011 entity records that are available for creation and modification. Once we select our entity, the default view for that entity will be displayed for us. We can create and edit the existing record. To create a new record, follow these steps:

1. Select the entity for which you need to create a record.
2. Click on the **New** button available in the default view window.
3. Enter the information in the selected fields.
4. Click on **Save**.

As soon as we save the record, it will be available with the **Edit** button and will link to **Related Entities**. We can create records for related entities if they are available to create and modify, as shown in the following screenshot:

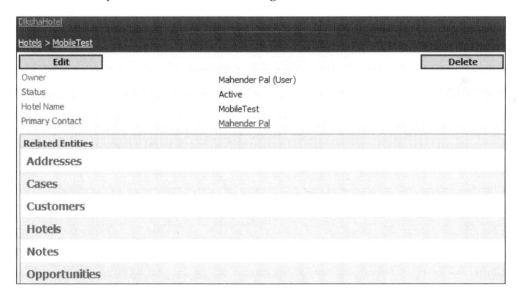

Other mobile solutions for Microsoft CRM 2011

Apart from OOB Mobile Express solutions, there are other mobile solutions available for Microsoft CRM 2011.

CWR Mobility

The **CWR Mobility** solution offers a mobile solution that provides a great deal of functionality, which is not available in Mobile Express. CWR Mobility supports different devices such as iPhone, iPad, Windows Phones, BlackBerry, and Android. CWR Mobility runs as a client on your phone. It provides us with several features, listed as follows:

- Familiar user experience: It provides a look and feel similar to Microsoft CRM 2011

- Native applications: It supports many devices such as Android, BlackBerry, iPod, iPhone

- Powerful integration with native device applications: It provides powerful integration with native device applications to access different types of data such as e-mail, contacts, and so on

- Role-based information delivery: It provides only specific information based on the user role

- Mobile dashboard: Provides support for all Microsoft CRM 2011 dashboards

- Mapping and navigation: Provides an easy way to locate customer addresses on the map

- Offline data support: You don't need to stay online all the time; it also supports offline data access

- Background synchronization: Easy synchronization when you are connected

- Multi device access: Multiple devices can be used to connect

- Easy deployment: Available in the market place and is easily deployed

We can request a trial from the CWR Mobility site, and if we have registered for a trial version for our Microsoft CRM 2011 online deployment, they will complete the installation for us. We just need to configure our customization according to our requirements. We can easily configure CWR using their configuration. We can access the CWR configuration by going to **Settings** | **CWR Mobile CRM**. We can easily add an entity that we want to expose to mobile devices, and configure data synchronization. We can also create or modify user profiles for mobile users.

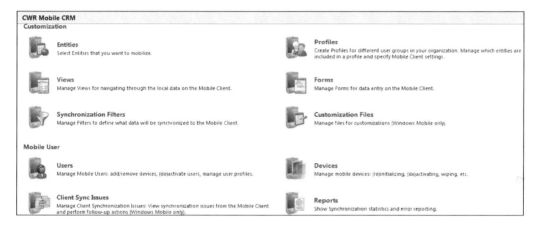

CWR Mobile also provides us with logs for all the activities done by CWR. It keeps all the auditing information that can help us to troubleshoot any issues, if they occur.

You can register for a free trial at http://www.cwrmobility.com/.

MobileAccess

MobileAccess is another mobile solution available in the market for Microsoft CRM 2011. MobileAccess have two solutions to support Microsoft CRM 2011 deployment:

- MobileAccess online
- MobileAccess on-premises

It provides variable key features such as multitasking support, GPS mapping, photo and multimedia capture and upload functionalities, advanced search and on-the-fly query creation, and document management. Some of the key features in this product are as follows:

- Offline data support: This feature provides offline data support
- Automated push synchronization: This feature provides automatic synchronization without any manual initiation
- Quick find: This feature provides quick find view support in offline mode
- Advanced search: This feature provides multiparameter search support
- Multitask with multiwindow navigation: With the help of this feature, we can use multiple windows simultaneously
- Workflow event notification: This feature provides notification support using workflow processes
- Multiple CRM record operations: This feature supports multiple operations on Microsoft CRM 2011 records, such as assigning records and viewing related records
- Appointment scheduling: This feature supports appointment scheduling in a remote manner
- Day/month calendar views: This feature provides multiple views for the calendar
- Copying and sharing CRM records: This feature supports sharing of records to non-CRM users
- GPS mapping: This feature supports capturing geo-coordinates on-the-fly
- Extended data types support: This feature provides additional data type support
- Embedded CRM workflows: This feature provides workflow operation support for specific entities
- Multimedia support: With the help of this feature, we can embed rich audio and visual information to Microsoft CRM 2011 records

We have taken references and screenshots for MobileAccess from `http://www.tendigits.com/about-mobile-crm.html`; you can refer to this location for more information on MobileAccess.

MobileAccess supports iPhone, BlackBerry, Android, Windows Mobile, and Windows Phone with Android, iPad, and BlackBerry Playbook tablet support. The **TenDigits MobileAccess** customization window is shown in the following screenshot:

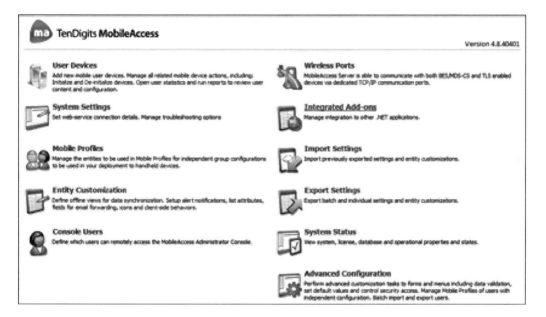

Mobile Edge for Microsoft Dynamics CRM on iPhone

Mobile Edge for Microsoft Dynamics CRM 2011 is another solution available for the iPhone. It provides easy access to Microsoft CRM 2011 from an iPhone. It uses a middleware server to connect Microsoft CRM 2011 using its web services. It provides options to deploy the middleware server in a client network or use a hosted middleware server deployment. The Mobile Edge solution used in an iPhone is shown in the following screenshot:

Mobile Edge is not a browser-based application; internally it uses a client-server architecture, which provides us complete online and offline capabilities when we are outside our network.

 We have taken references and screenshots for Mobile Edge from `http://www.ienterprises.com/products/mobile-edge/mobile-edge-for-ms-dynamics-on-iphone.html`; you can refer to this location for more information on Mobile Edge.

Resco Mobile CRM

Resco Mobile CRM is another mobile solution available for Microsoft CRM 2011 on the market. It supports all mobile devices such as Android, iPhone, iPad, and Windows Phone. It does not use any middleware or server component. You just need to download the application and install it. The following screenshot gives a view of the dashboards, which is one of the features of Resco Mobile:

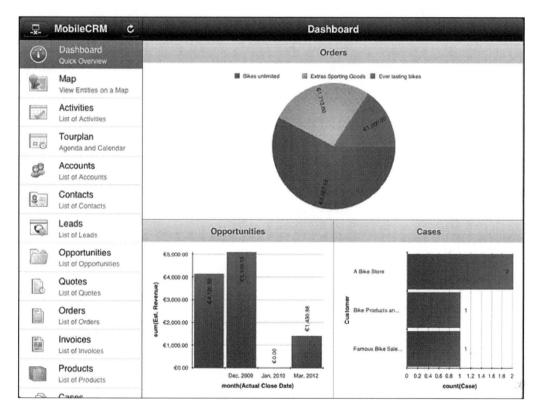

It provides a configuration tool along with a rich platform-independent SDK to customize mobile application based on the requirement.

We have taken references and screenshots for Resco Mobile CRM from http://www.resco.net/; you can refer to this location for more information on Mobile Edge.

Summary

In this chapter we learned about mobile clients for Microsoft CRM 2011. We learned about Mobile Express features in Microsoft CRM 2011, and how to expose entities for Mobile Express. We finally learned how to create and customize mobile entity forms and how to set up fields in mobile forms. We also discussed mobile solutions available in the market for Microsoft CRM 2011.

In the next chapter we learn how to create an issue-tracker application.

8
Issue Tracker Using Microsoft CRM 2011

In this chapter, we are going to create an Issue Tracker application using Microsoft CRM 2011 as the platform. In this chapter, you will learn how to create a plugin and a custom workflow using Visual Studio 2010. We will discuss the following points in this chapter:

- Issue Tracker basics
- Application scope
- Issue Manager design
- Customizing Microsoft CRM 2011 for Issue Manager
- Setting up a security roles
- Plugin to generate an auto ID
- Plugin versus custom workflow assembly
- Issue assignment workflow
- Working with custom workflows
- Sending notifications using workflows
- Creating the Issue Manager dashboard
- Testing

Issue Tracker basics

The Issue Tracker application is used to create and manage issues. It plays an important part in application development. An Issue Tracker system helps us to manage different projects at the same time. A good issue tracker can help us provide a 360-degree view of the issue resolution process. We can easily track the status of the issue submitted. Once the issue is submitted, it is assigned to the appropriate resources for resolution.

The features of Issue Tracker application are as follows:

- Searching by project, assigned person, priority, and status
- Sorting by columns (either issue ID, project, priority, assigned person, or status)
- Administration of users
- Administration of priorities
- Administration of projects
- Administration of statuses

We can use Microsoft CRM 2011 to develop issue tracker, and we can implement all these requirements easily by customizing and extending Microsoft CRM 2011.

Application scope

We are going to use Microsoft CRM 2011 to create an issue manager. We will be using the OOB functionality of Microsoft CRM 2011 to design our application. We will use the on-premise deployment of Microsoft CRM 2011 for our application. The QA resource can access our application to submit an issue manually. We will write custom logic, which will fire on creation of the issue. This issue will be assigned to the team member who's currently working on fewer issues. The assignment of issues is decided by the project team selected while creating the issue.

We will create another workflow to send a notification when a case is assigned to a resource. For example, we need to send a notification to a team member or to the QA resource when the issue is assigned to the team member.

Issue Manager design

We are going to create an issue and project for three custom entities. We will use the Issue entity to capture information regarding the issue, for example, the issue description, category, created date, and submitted by date, along with error reproducing steps. The Project entity will be used to store project-related information. We will create a 1:N relationship between the project and issue. We are going to create another custom entity, namely Auto ID Setup. We will use this entity to store auto ID configuration information. We will write a plugin to generate an issue ID using auto ID setup configuration.

The following block diagram is the entity design for Issue Manager:

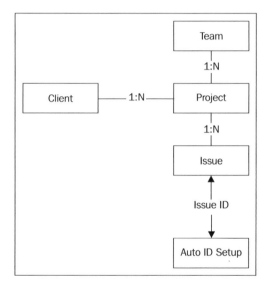

We are going to use the OOB Account entity to store client information. There could be different projects for the same client so there is a 1:N relationship between the Client and Project entities. We will use the Team entity to track group consultants who will be working on particular projects based on their respective technologies.

Customizing Microsoft CRM 2011 for Issue Manager

Now we have an understanding of our application scope and design, let's start customizing Microsoft CRM 2011.

Creating custom entities and their attributes

Let's create our custom solution and name it `IssueManager`. (Please refer to *Chapter 2, Customizing Microsoft Dynamics CRM 2011*, to create a Solution in Microsoft CRM 2011).

Perform the following steps to create the Issue entity:

1. Open the `IssueManager` solution.
2. Navigate to **Components | Entities | New**.
3. Enter the following information:
   - **Display Name**: Issue
   - **Plural Name**: Issues
   - **Ownership**: User or Team
   - **Area that display this entity**: Workplace
   - **Communication & Collaboration**: Check the **Notes & Activities** checkbox only
4. Click on **Save** to create the entity.

Now we have created the entity, so let's add an attribute to the Issue entity. Please refer to *Appendix A, Data Model*, for the Issue entity data model. Once the attribute is created/modified, we need to place our fields on the entity form. Open the main entity form and double-click on the fields to place them on the form. Once done, our issue form should look like the following screenshot:

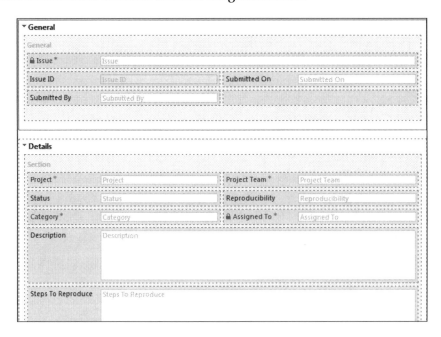

Now, we need to create views for open and close issues; perform the following steps to create a view for an open issue:

1. Navigate to **Views** and click on **New**.

2. Enter `Open Issues` in the **Name** field and `view for open issue` in the **Description** field.

3. Click on **Add Columns** to add the required columns, and the view should look like the following screenshot:

4. Click on **Edit Filter Criteria** to add a filter condition.

5. Filter criteria should look like the following screenshot:

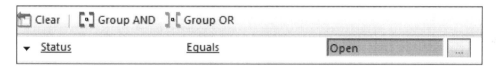

6. Click on **Save and Close**.

  You can hide the entity views of Microsoft CRM 2011 by deactivating them if you don't want to use them.

In the same way, we can set up views for other statuses as well.

Now let's create our Project entity; use the following information to create the Project entity:

- **Display Name**: Project
- **Plural Name**: Projects
- **Ownership**: User or Team
- **Area that display this entity**: Workplace
- **Communication & Collaboration**: Check the **Notes & Activities** checkbox only

Please see *Appendix A, Data Model*, for the Project entity data model to create attributes for the Project entity and place them on the main form. Our project entity form should look like the following screenshot:

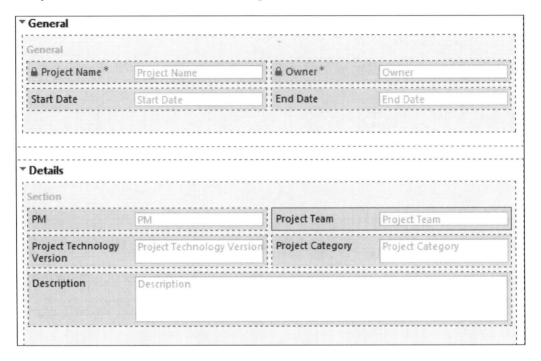

Now let's create our Auto ID Setup entity. Use the following information to create the Auto ID Setup entity:

- **Display Name**: Auto ID Setup
- **Plural Name**: Auto ID Setups
- **Ownership**: User or Team
- **Area that display this entity**: Workplace
- **Communication & Collaboration**: Uncheck all selected checkboxes

Please see *Appendix A, Data Model*, for the Project entity data model to create attributes for the Auto ID Setup entity and place them on the main form. Our Auto ID Setup entity form should look like the following screenshot:

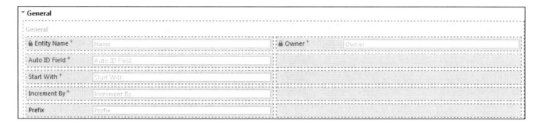

Setting up security roles

For our application, we will create the following two security roles:

- QA
- Developer

The QA security role will be assigned to all QA resources and the developer security role will be assigned to team members. We can rename existing security roles or create new roles by copying existing roles. A sales person role is the most suitable security role because they have most of the permission granted that we need for our QA and developer resources. So we can use them to create our QA and developer security roles, and modify them to remove unnecessary permissions.

 The best practice to create a new role is to copy an existing role instead of creating a new one from scratch.

So let's create a QA and developer security role by copying the security roles of the sales persons and removing the following entity permissions from the respective roles. You can refer to *Chapter 2, Customizing Microsoft Dynamics CRM 2011*, for details on creating a new security role.

Modify QA and developer roles based on the following table:

Area	Description
Sales, Marketing, Service	Remove all permissions from all entities in the respective area
Core Area	Remove all permissions from Contact, Customer Relationship, Lead, Opportunity, Opportunity Relationship, Relationship Role, Subject, Document location, E-mail Template, Mail Merge Template, SharePoint Site, Data map, and Data Import
Client, Project	Remove Create permission for these entities, under **Custom Entities** tab
Auto ID Setup, Issue, Project	Add Organization access for all the permissions, except Create for Project entity

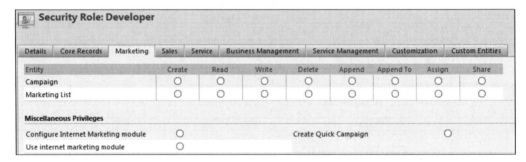

Now we have our customization ready, so let's apply business logic for our application. We need to apply the following business logic:

- Generate an auto issue ID while a new issue is being created
- Auto assign an issue to the team member who has been assigned the fewest issues
- Send a notification to the team member and Project Manager when new issue is assigned to the team member

Plugin to generate auto ID

Now let's write a plugin to generate an auto ID. Generating an auto ID in Microsoft CRM is a very common requirement. So we are going to write a generic plugin to generate an auto ID for any entity. We have created an Auto ID Setup entity, which we will use to create the entity record for which we need to generate an auto ID. We will specify the entity name and auto ID field name, and we will use this information in our plugin to set the auto ID.

First we will create an Auto ID Setup entity record that will provide an entity name, auto ID field, and start number for generating an issue ID. Create an auto ID setup record and enter the following information:

- **Name**: new_issue
- **Auto ID Field**: new_issuenumber
- **Start with**: You can enter any number as a starting point
- **Increment By**: Enter any positive number
- **Prefix**: If you want to add a prefix before the issue ID, you can use this field

In *Chapter 4, Implementing Business Logic through Plugin*, we used Developer Toolkit to write a plugin. In this chapter, I will explain how to write a plugin without using Developer Toolkit. Perform the following steps to create a plugin assembly in Visual Studio 2010:

1. Start Visual Studio 2010 and go to **File | New | Project | Visual C#**.
2. Select the **Class Library** template and name it `Generate_AutoID`.
3. Rename `Class1.cs` as `AutoID.cs`.
4. Go to the **Signing** tab and check the **Sign the assembly** checkbox.
5. Right-click on the `Project` folder and select **Add Reference...** to add a reference for the following assemblies:
    ○ `Microsoft.xrm.sdk`
    ○ `System.Runtime.Serialization`
6. Open the `AutoID.cs` file.
7. Add the following `using` directive to our class:
```
using Microsoft.Xrm.Sdk;
using Microsoft.Xrm.Sdk.Query;
```
8. We need to write the following two functions in our class apart from the main plugin `Execute` function:
    ○ `GetAutoIDSetupDetails`: This function is used to get details from the Auto ID Setup entity
    ○ `GetAutoNumber`: This function is used to generate an auto ID number

First, we need to write a function to get auto ID setup details. This is required to read the **Start With** number, to assign an issue number, and increment it with the value present in the **Increment By** field. Our query expression should look like the following code snippet:

```
Entity Autoidsetup = null;
        QueryExpression _Query = new QueryExpression
        {
            EntityName = "new_autoidsetup",
            ColumnSet = new ColumnSet("new_incrementby", "new_
prefix", "new_startwith", "new_name", "new_autoidsetupid", "new_
autoidfield"),
            Criteria =
            {
                FilterOperator = LogicalOperator.And,
                Conditions =
                    {
                        new ConditionExpression
                        {
                            AttributeName="new_name",
                            Operator=ConditionOperator.Equal,
                            Values={EntityName}
                        }
                    }
            }
        };
        EntityCollection EntitiesColleciton = service.
RetrieveMultiple(_Query);
if (EntitiesColleciton.Entities.Count > 0)
        {
            Autoidsetup = EntitiesColleciton.Entities.First();
        }
        return Autoidsetup;
```

 As we are using the late bound programming style here, we need to make sure that we are using the logical name of the fields.

In the previous method, we have used the `QueryExpression` class to query the Auto ID Setup entity to read a record based on the entity name in which the current plugin is being executed. Once we get the result, we need to get the first entity object from the entity collection and return it to the calling function.

After getting an auto ID number, we need to assign that number to the **Issue Number** field. We want to generate the auto ID at the time of record creation so that we have an option to register our plugin as either precreate or postcreate. If we will register our plugin as postcreate, we need to write an update request to update **Auto ID Field** after record creation. But if we register our plugin as precreate, we can inject the **Auto ID Field** property in the property bag of the entity before record creation; so, we are going to register our plugin as precreate. Let's add our Execute method in our plugin class, where we can get a plugin context to get entity information and add an attribute to the entity property collection. Our code should look as follows:

```
IPluginExecutionContext context = (IPluginExecutionContext)
serviceProvider.GetService(typeof(IPluginExecutionContext));
            Entity PrimaryEntity;
            if (context.InputParameters.Contains("Target") &&
            context.InputParameters["Target"] is Entity)
            {
                PrimaryEntity = (Entity)context.
InputParameters["Target"];
            }
            else
            { return; }
            IOrganizationServiceFactory serviceFactory =
(IOrganizationServiceFactory)serviceProvider.GetService(typeof(IOrgani
zationServiceFactory));
            IOrganizationService service = serviceFactory.CreateOrgani
zationService(context.UserId);
            try
            {
                if (context.MessageName == "Create")
                {
                    Entity Autosetupdetails = GetAutoIDSetupDetails(Pr
imaryEntity.LogicalName, service);
                    if (Autosetupdetails != null)
                    {
                        if (Autosetupdetails.Contains("new_
autoidfield"))
                        {
                            string AutoIDFieldName =
Autosetupdetails["new_autoidfield"].ToString();
                            PrimaryEntity.Attributes.
Add(AutoIDFieldName, GetAutoNumber(service, Autosetupdetails).
ToString());
                        }
                    }
                    else
                        return;
                }
```

In the preceding code, we have retrieved the primary entity from the context and passed the entity name to the `GetAutoIDSetupDetails` function to fetch the Auto ID Setup entity record based on the entity name. If it returns a record, we will use that record to generate our auto ID; otherwise we will cancel the execution of the plugin by returning a control.

You can find complete code under `Code\Generate_AutoID` for this chapter.

Perform the following steps to build a plugin assembly and register it using the plugin registration tool:

1. Open `PluginRegistration.exe` and connect to your organization, as shown in the following screenshot:

2. Once you are connected to your organization, it will display all the plugins registered for your organization.

3. Navigate to **Register** and select the **Register New Assembly** option, as shown in the following screenshot:

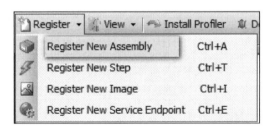

4. Browse your assembly using the default settings.

5. Click on **Register Selected Plugins**.

6. Select your plugin assembly and navigate to **Register | Register New Step**. We need to use the information shown in the following screenshot when registering the **Create** step:

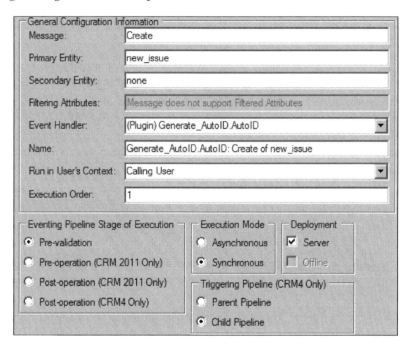

7. After registration, the plugin assembly should look like the following screenshot:

Plugin versus custom workflow assembly

We need to implement business logic to assign an issue to the team member who has been assigned with the fewest issues. This requirement can't be implemented using the OOB functionality; however, we can develop custom business logic using a different option. The two main options are to use a plugin or a custom workflow. Both options can be used to implement business requirements based on the developers' choices and the requirement details. The plugins and custom workflows have their own features. We can review these differences in the following table:

Plugin	Custom workflow
A plugin can either be executed synchronously or asynchronously.	A workflow can be executed asynchronously only.
A plugin is supported on all deployment models.	A custom workflow is supported only on on-premise deployment.
Configuration or medication of a plugin requires a technical resource.	Once a custom workflow is written by a technical resource, a non-technical resource can configure the workflow using CRM UI.
A plugin is most suitable when we need a response without any delay.	A workflow is the best option when there might be a delay in the result.
A plugin supports multiple event. We can refer Message entity support for plugins to get all supported events. This file comes with Microsoft CRM 2011 SDK.	A workflow can be configured for some specific event available in the workflow designer.
We can register images in a plugin.	We cannot register an image for a workflow.

 Very soon, we are going to get a Microsoft CRM 2011 service update, which will allow us to write a custom workflow for Microsoft CRM 2011 online as well. You can refer to http://gustafwesterlund.blogspot.in/2012/04/workflow-activities-in-crm-online.html for more information on this.

Issue assignment process

Based on the previously discussed differences, I am going to develop a custom workflow to implement this requirement. The following screenshot shows the workflow process diagram that we need to implement:

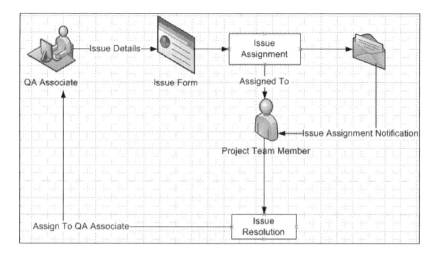

When a QA associate creates an issue record, he will add basic information related to the issue. He will also select the project team in the project team member lookup. Once he saves the issue record, we will start the issue assignment workflow. The issue assignment process will find out the team member who has the least issues assigned and assign the issue to that member. Once the issue is assigned, our workflow will send a notification to the concerned team member about the issue assignment.

Working with custom workflows

Microsoft CRM 2011 provides a very rich OOB workflow UI designer that we can use to create our workflow, to implement our business logic. But if there is a complex requirement that cannot be implemented using the OOB workflow, we can create a custom workflow. We have two options to create a custom workflow; we can either write a custom workflow assembly or we can create a custom XAML workflow. In our sample application, we are going to write a custom workflow assembly. You can refer to `http://technet.microsoft.com/en-us/library/gg309458.aspx` to create a custom XAML workflow.

We can use Windows Workflow Foundation to create the custom workflow activities. Windows Workflow Foundation provides us with an activity library, which includes activities for control flow, sending and receiving messages, and doing work in parallel.

At present, the custom workflow assembly is supported only in on-premise versions, but very soon we are going to get a Microsoft CRM 2011 service update that will allow us to write the custom workflow for Microsoft CRM 2011 online as well.

Let's discuss the custom workflow concept:

- **Workflow context**: In the custom workflow, we need to override the Execute method that takes CodeActivityContext as a parameter. We can get a workflow context from CodeActivityContext, which can later be used to create a service object and to get entity-specific conceptual information. We can use the following code to initiate the workflow context:

```
IWorkflowContext context=executionContext.GetExtension
<IWorkflowContext>();
IOrganizationServiceFactory serviceFactory =
executionContext.GetExtension<IOrganizationServiceFactory>();
IOrganizationService service =
serviceFactory.CreateOrganizationService(context.
InitiatingUserId);
```

- **Parameters**: The workflow supports arguments that we can use, to send information in or out. We can use the following three types of arguments:
  - In
  - Out
  - InOut

  We can use the In argument to pass data to the workflow activity, and we can use the Out argument to send data from the workflow activity. The InOut argument can be used for both purposes. We can define an argument in our custom workflow activity by using properties of the InArgument, OutArgument, and InOutArgument types.

  We can declare an argument variable, as shown in the following code snippet:

```
[Input("Prompt for User")]
[Default("datatype specific value")]
public InArgument<Datatypeofinputparameter> Nameofinputvariable
{get;set;}
```

- **Input**: This is the display label that will be displayed to the user
- **Default**: We can specify a default value based on the input variable datatype
- **InArgument**: This is the property for the input argument

- **Input variables**:

  The input variables are used to pass information to workflow assembly. The following examples are to declare the input variable for the different datatypes:

  ○ **String**:

  The following code snippet is an example for the string datatype:

  ```
  [Input("Please Enter Student Name")]
  [Default("Name")]
  public InArgument<string> SName {get;set;}
  ```

  ○ **Double**:

  The following code snippet is an example for the double datatype:

  ```
  [Input("Enter Cost")]
  public InArgument<double>Cost{get;set;}
  ```

- **Output variables**:

  In the same way, we can declare an output argument, as shown in the following code snippet:

  ```
  [Output("Prompt for output")]
  public OutArgument<Datatypeofoutputparameter> Nameofoutputvariable
  {get;set;}
  ```

  The following is an example for an output variable:

  ```
  [Output("Total Cost")]
  public OutArgument<double>Totalcost {get;set;}
  ```

- **InOutArgument**:

  The InOutArgument parameter can be declared, as shown in the following code snippet:

  ```
  [Input("Total Value")]
  [Output("Total Value Result")]
  public InOutArgument<decimal>TotalCost {get;set;}
  ```

Now we have a basic understanding of a custom workflow, so let's write our custom workflow to assign an issue.

Perform the following steps to create a custom workflow activity library:

1. Start Visual Studio 2010 and go to **File | New | Project | Visual C#**.

2. Go to **Workflow | Activity Library** and name it `Issueassignment`.

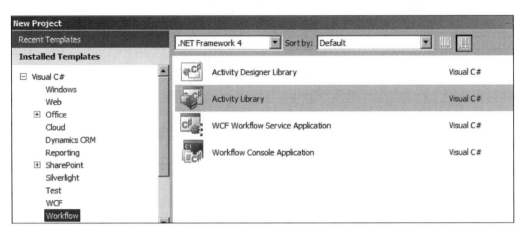

3. Delete the `Activity.xaml` file under **Solution Explorer**.

4. Right-click on the `Project` folder, select **Add | New Item**, and add a new class named `AssignIssue.cs`.

5. Right-click on the `Project` folder and select **Property**, and make sure **.NET Framework 4** is selected under **Target framework**, as shown in the following screenshot:

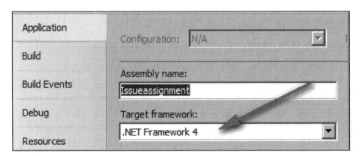

6. Right-click on the `Project` folder and select **Add Reference...** to add a reference for the following assemblies:

```
Microsoft.Xrm.Sdk.Workflow;
Microsoft.Xrm.Sdk;
Microsoft.Crm.Sdk.Messages;
System.Runtime.Serialization
```

7. Go to the **Signing** tab and check the **Sign the assembly** checkbox.

8. Open the `AssignIssue.cs` file to start adding code.

   Add the following code snippet with the `using` directive to your class:

```
using Microsoft.Xrm.Sdk.Query;
using System.Activities;
using Microsoft.Xrm.Sdk.Workflow;
using Microsoft.Xrm.Sdk;
using Microsoft.Crm.Sdk.Messages;
```

We have the following three main requirements for our custom workflow:

1. Find all the members of the team assigned to the current issue.

2. Find the team member who has the fewest issues assigned.

3. Assign an issue to the team member who has the fewest issues assigned.

Find all members of the team

We can't get team members from a single entity, so we need to write a query to join two entities to fetch team members, and then we can pass that query to the `RetrieveMultiple` method of the Iorganizaiton web service. We can join the `systemuser` and `teammembership` entities to fetch all the team members. To fetch the team members of a specified team, we should use the following code:

```
EntityCollection _Teammembers = null;
        Guid _UserId = Guid.Empty;
        EntityCollection col = new EntityCollection();
        QueryExpression _Query = new QueryExpression();
        _Query.EntityName = "systemuser";
    _Query.ColumnSet = new ColumnSet(new string[] {
"systemuserid", "firstname" });
        LinkEntity _LinkEntity = new LinkEntity();
        _LinkEntity.LinkFromAttributeName = "systemuserid";
        _LinkEntity.LinkToAttributeName = "systemuserid";
        _LinkEntity.LinkFromEntityName = "systemuser";
        _LinkEntity.LinkToEntityName = "teammembership";
        _LinkEntity.JoinOperator = JoinOperator.Natural;
        _LinkEntity.LinkCriteria = new FilterExpression();
        _LinkEntity.LinkCriteria.AddCondition("teamid",
ConditionOperator.Equal, TeamID);
        _Query.LinkEntities.Add(_LinkEntity);
        _Teammembers = _Service.RetrieveMultiple(_Query);
```

Find the team member with fewest issues assigned

Once we have the entity collection of the team member, we can find the team member who has the fewest issues assigned, by looping through the entity collection. We need to apply two conditions to get a user. Our first condition will be to compare the owner ID of the issue, and another condition will be to check only for the project assigned in the issue record. As we need to check conditions other than the primary field, we need to use the `RetrieveMultiple` function to fetch user's record. Our code should be as follows:

```
Guid _LeastIssueAssignedUserID = Guid.Empty;
        int _IssueCount = 0;
        int _MinimumIssueCount = -1;
        foreach(Entity Memeber in _Teammember.Entities)
        {
            QueryExpression _Query = new QueryExpression();
            _Query.EntityName = "new_issue";
            _Query.ColumnSet = new ColumnSet();
            _Query.ColumnSet.AddColumn("new_name");
            _Query.Criteria = new FilterExpression();
            _Query.Criteria.FilterOperator = LogicalOperator.And;
            ConditionExpression condition1 = new Condition
Expression("ownerid",ConditionOperator.Equal,new Guid(Memeber.
Attributes["systemuserid"].ToString()));
            ConditionExpression condition2 = new
ConditionExpression("new_project", ConditionOperator.Equal,
ProjectID);
            _Query.Criteria.Conditions.AddRange(condition1,
condition2);
            EntityCollection Issues = _Service.RetrieveMultiple(_
Query);
            //get Issue count
            _IssueCount = Issues.Entities.Count;

            if (_MinimumIssueCount == -1)
            {
                _MinimumIssueCount = _IssueCount;
                _LeastIssueAssignedUserID = new Guid(Memeber.
Attributes["systemuserid"].ToString());
            }
            if (_IssueCount<_MinimumIssueCount)
            {
```

```
                    _MinimumIssueCount = _IssueCount;
                    _LeastIssueAssignedUserID = new Guid(Memeber.
Attributes["systemuserid"].ToString());
                    }



        }
```

Assign an issue to the team member with fewest issues assigned

Once we have an user who has the fewest issues assigned, we can write an assign request to assign an issue to that user. We need to pass our assign request to the `Execute` method of the IOrganizaiton web service. Our code should be as follows:

```
AssignRequest _Request = new AssignRequest
                {                       Assignee = new
EntityReference("systemuser", MemberID),
                    Target = new EntityReference("new_issue", IssueID)
                };


            AssignResponse _Response = (AssignResponse)_Service.
Execute(_Request);
```

Now let's add the `Execute` method to our custom activity class. Use the following code for the `Execute` method. First we need to get the context for Microsoft CRM 2011 from the `codeActivityContext` object. Once we have the context, we can get entity information from this context. We need to retrieve our primary entity ID so that we can query an issue record based on that ID. We need to retrieve the project team assigned to this issue.

```
protected override void Execute(CodeActivityContext Execution)
        {
            IWorkflowContext context = Execution.GetExtension<IWorkfl
owContext>();
            IOrganizationServiceFactory serviceFactory =
            Execution.GetExtension<IOrganizationServiceFactory>();
            IOrganizationService service =serviceFactory.CreateOrganiz
ationService(context.InitiatingUserId);
            Guid IssueID = context.PrimaryEntityId;
            Entity _Issue = (Entity)service.Retrieve("new_issue",
IssueID, new ColumnSet(new string[] {"new_project","new_projectteam"
})));
```

```
              Guid _LeastIssueAssignedUser=GetTeamUser(servi
ce, ((EntityReference)_Issue.Attributes["new_projectteam"]).Id,
((EntityReference)_Issue.Attributes["new_project"]).Id);
              AssignIssueToUser(_LeastIssueAssignedUser, IssueID,
service);
          }
```

> Note that you can find the complete code under Code\
> Issueassignment.

Now our code is complete. So let's build our assembly and register it.

> Refer to the *Plugin to generate auto ID* section to register
> the assembly only; we can't register the step for the
> custom workflow.

Workflow to assign an issue to a team member

Now we have our custom workflow in place, so let's design our workflow to assign an issue to a team member based on the number of issues assigned to him. Perform the following steps to create a workflow:

1. Navigate to **Setting | Processes | New**.
2. Enter the following information on the workflow dialog box and click on **OK**:
   1. **Process Name: Issue Assignment**
   2. **Entity: Issue**
   3. **Category: Workflow**
   4. **Type: New Blank Process**
3. Set **Scope** to **Organization** and set **Start when** to **Record is created**.
4. Click on **Add Step** and select our custom workflow assembly.

Once done, our workflow should look like the following screenshot:

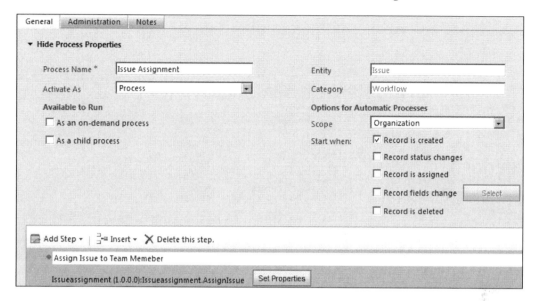

5.   Click on **Save and Close** and activate the workflow.

Sending notifications using workflows

We need to send an issue assignment notification to the assigned member.
We can create a workflow to send the notification and set it to run when the
record is assigned.

Perform the following steps to create the workflow to send a notification:

1.   Navigate to **Setting | Processes | New**.

2.   Enter the following information on the workflow dialog box and click on **OK**:

   1.   **Process Name**: Send Issue Assignment Notification

   2.   **Entity**: Issue

   3.   **Category**: Workflow

   4.   **Type**: New Blank Process

3.   Set **Scope** to **Organization** and set **Start when** to **Record is assigned**.

4.   Select **Add Step | Send E-mail** and click on the **Set Properties** button.

5. Select the **From** field and select **Modified By** from **Form Assistant**:

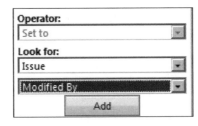

6. Click on **Add** and then click on the **OK** button.

7. In the same way, set **Assigned To** from **Form Assistant** in the **To** field.

8. In the **Subject** field, enter `Issue :<<Issue ID>> is assigned to you.`

    We need to provide an issue record link to the user in the **Description** field of the e-mail so that the team member can directly click on that to open the issue record.

9. Select the **Insert Hyperlink** option from the e-mail description toolbar, set the properties as shown in the following screenshot, and click on **OK**:

Once done, our e-mail should look like the following screenshot:

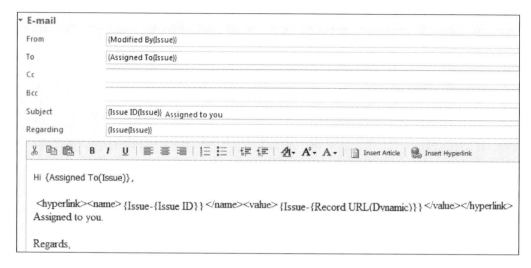

10. Click on **Save and Close** and activate the workflow.

Creating the Issue Manager dashboard

We have created the issue assignment workflow that will assign the issue to the team member who has the fewest issues assigned. So let's design our Issue Manager dashboard so issue management can be tracked easily. Perform the following steps to create our Issue Manager dashboard:

1. Open the `IssueManager` solution and navigate to **Components | Entities | Issue**.

2. Select **View** and click on **New**.

3. Enter the following information in the **View** properties:
    - **Name**: My Issues
    - **Description**: List of the issue assigned to me

4. Click on **Add Columns** and add the columns that we added while creating the Open Issue view.

5. Click on **Edit Filter Criteria**, as shown in the following screenshot, and click on **OK**:

6. Click on **Save and Close**.

We have created a view based on the current user; now let's create a chart control based on the My Issues view.

Introduction to charts in Microsoft CRM 2011

Microsoft CRM 2011 has introduced a new feature to create charts for a single entity view. Charts help us to graphically represent our organization's data effectively. We can use charts to display information in two axes, horizontal (X) and vertical (Y). The horizontal axis can be used to display numerical as well as non-numerical values, whereas the vertical axis can be used to display only numeric values. We can create the following different charts in Microsoft CRM 2011:

- Bar
- Column
- Funnel
- Line
- Pie

Microsoft CRM 2011 allows us to create two types of charts, namely system charts and user charts. System charts are available to all Microsoft CRM 2011 users, while user charts can be accessed by other CRM users if they are shared or assigned to them.

Let's create our chart with the following steps:

1. Select **Charts** and click on **New**.
2. Select the **My Issues** view from the view drop-down menu.
3. Enter the chart name as My Issues Chart.
4. Select the **Pie** chart from the **Chart** group in the ribbon toolbar.
5. Select the **Status** field from **Legend Entries**, and **Count All** from the **Aggregate** drop-down menu.

6. Select **Status** from the **Horizontal (Category) Axis Labels** drop-down menu.

Once done, our chart should look like the following screenshot:

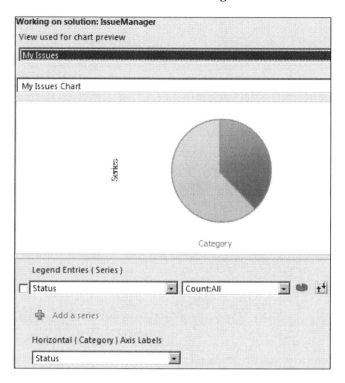

Now we have our view and chart ready so let's create our dashboard and place the **My Issues** list and chart on it.

Perform the following steps to set up the dashboard:

1. Navigate to **Workplace | My Work | Dashboard** on the CRM home page.

2. Click on **New** and select **2- Column Regular Dashboard**, and click on **Create**.

3. Enter `Issue Manager` under the **Name** section.

4. Remove existing components and click on **List** in the ribbon toolbar.

5. Select **Issue** in **Record Type** and **My Issue** in **View**.

6. Click on the **Chart** button on the ribbon toolbar, and select **Issue** in **Record Type**, **My Issue** in **View**, and **My Issue Chart** from the **Chart** drop-down menu.

7. Click on **Save and Close**.

Now our application is ready for testing. The System Administrator can start creating the project and set up development teams. Once the testing resource starts entering the issue, the workflow will start working and assign an issue based on the workflow logic that we developed.

Once the developers start working on the issues, their dashboard should like the following screenshot:

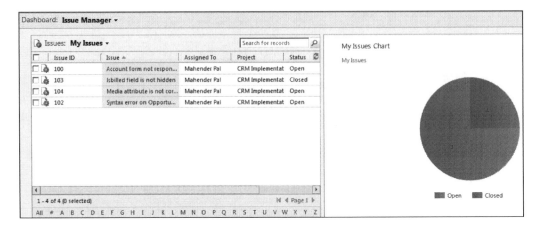

The e-mail notification sent to the team member will look like the following screenshot:

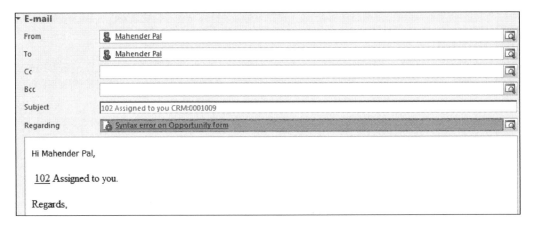

Summary

In this chapter, we learned the basics of the Issue Tracker application. We learned to map the Microsoft CRM 2011 application to fulfill the requirement of the Issue Tracker application. We learned how to create an Issue Tracker application using the features of Microsoft CRM 2011 OOB. We learned how to write a plugin to generate an auto ID setup. We learned to develop a custom workflow. We learned to create chart control and place it on the dashboard.

A
Data Model

Data model

OOB data model	Customized	Renamed to	Business level
Entity name: Account	**Yes**	**Institute**	
Attribute list			
Category	Yes	Institute type, modify label (Preferred customer: Head office, Standard: Branch office)	
Account name	Yes	Institute name	Required
Address 1: City	Yes	City	Required
Address 1: Country/ Region	Yes	Country/Region	Required
Address 1: Fax	Yes	Fax	
Address 1: Street 1	Yes	Address 1	Required
Address 1: Street 2	Yes	Address 2	
Address 1: Street 3	Yes	Address 3	
Address 1: ZIP/Postal code	Yes	ZIP code	
Telephone1	Yes	Main phone	Required
Address1_Telephone2	Yes	Help desk contact	Required
Parent account	Yes	Head office	
Website	Yes	Website	
E-mail	No	E-mail	

Entity name: Contact		Student	
Attribute list			
Salutation	No		
First name	No		Required
Last name	No		Required
Birthday	No		
Gender	No		
Marital status	No		
Parent customer	Yes	Enrolled at	Required
Middle name	Yes	Father's name	
Preferred contact method	Yes	Course (Add new options:DIC,DIAC, PGDCA,MCA,MSc Computers,BSc Computers,BCA, BE,Btech)	Required
Address 1: City	Yes	City	
Address 1: Country/ Region	Yes	Country/Region	
Address 1: County	Yes	County	
Address 1: Fax	Yes	Fax	
Address 1: Street 1	Yes	Address 1	Required
Address 1: Street 2	Yes	Address 2	
Address 1: ZIP/Postal Code	Yes	ZIP/Postal code	
Address 1: Post office box	Yes	Post office box	
Address 1: State/ Province	Yes	State/Province	
Telephone1	Yes	Home phone	Required
Address1_Telephone2	Yes	Mobile	Required
E-mail	No		Required

B

Hotel Entity Data Model and Design

We have used the Account entity to store hotel information. The Hotel entity will contain information about the rooms in the hotel, so we have created some new fields in the entity. The following tables show the data model for the Hotel entity:

Field name	Display name	Type	Custom attribute	Comments
Name	Hotel Name	String	False	Format: Text Maximum length: 160

Room entity data model

The Room entity will store information about the room category and facilities available in that room. The following table shows the data model for the Room entity:

Field name	Display name	Type	Custom attribute	Comments
new_lcd	LCD	Boolean	True	True: Yes False: No Default value: Yes

Field name	Display name	Type	Custom attribute	Comments
new_freepickdrop	Free Pick & Drop	Boolean	True	True: Yes
				False: No
				Default value: Yes
new_phone	Phone	Integer	True	Minimum value: 0
				Maximum value: 15
new_wifi	Wifi	Boolean	True	True: Yes
				False: No
				Default value: Yes
new_status	Status	Picklist	True	Options:
				100000000: Booked
				100000001: Available
				Default: -1
new_morningtea	Morning Tea	Boolean	True	True: Yes
				False: No
				Default value: Yes
new_ breakfastdinner	Breakfast & Dinner	Boolean	True	True: Yes
				False: No
				Default value: Yes
new_ laundryservice	Laundry service	Boolean	True	True: Yes
				False: No
				Default value: Yes
new_ bookingenddate	Booking End Date	DateTime	True	Format: Date only

Field name	Display name	Type	Custom attribute	Comments
new_ bookingstartdate	Booking Start Date	DateTime	True	Format: Date only
new_roomtypeid	Room Type	Lookup	True	Targets: Product
new_ parenthotelid	Parent Hotel	Lookup	True	Targets: Account
new_newspaper	Newspaper	Boolean	True	True: Yes False: No Default value: Yes
new_room_no	Room_no	String	True	Format: Text Maximum length: 100
new_maxguests	Max Guests	Picklist	True	Options: 100000000: 1 100000001: 2 100000002: 3 Default: -1
Ownerid	Owner	Owner	False	
new_hairdryer	Hair dryer	Boolean	True	True: Yes False: No Default value: Yes
new_ airconditioning	Air conditioning	Boolean	True	True: Yes False: No Default value: Yes

Food entity data model

The Food entity will store information about the food items ordered by the customer. We have created an N:1 relationship between the Food and Contact entities.

Field name	Display name	Type	Custom attribute	Comments
new_orderdate	Order Date	DateTime	True	Format: Date only
new_cost	Cost	Money	True	Minimum value: 0
				Maximum value: 1000000000
				Precision: 4
new_menu	Menu	Picklist	True	Options:
				1: Tea
				2: Coffee
				3: Vegetable Pakora
				4: Samosa
				5: Aaloo tikki
				6: Chicken Pakora
				7: Roti
				8: Paratha
				9: Chicken Curry
				10: Chicken Makhni
				11: Rajmah Masala
				12: Karhi Pakora
				13: Chicken Biryani
				14: Daal Makhni
				15: Chicken Biryani
				16: Jeera Rice
				17: Cold Drink
				18: Mineral water
				Default: -1

Field name	Display name	Type	Custom attribute	Comments
new_name	Name	String	True	Format: Text Maximum length: 100
new_ quantity	Quantity	Integer	True	Minimum value: 0 Maximum value: 50

Customer entity data model

We are using the Contact entity to store customer information. In the Customer entity, we need to store the customer's basic information. We need to store the room details and food items ordered by that customer. The following table shows the new fields that we have created for the Customer entity:

Field Name	Display Name	Type	Custom Attribute	Comments
new_roomdetailsid	Room Details	Lookup	True	Targets: New room
new_checkout	Check Out	DateTime	True	Format: Date only
new_checkin	Check In	DateTime	True	Format: Date only

Product entity data model

We have used the Product entity to store room service information. We have not created any new fields in the Product entity. We are using all OOB fields with little customization:

Field name	Display name	Type	Custom attribute	Comments
Product type code	Product Type	Picklist	False	Options: 1: Deluxe 2: Deluxe Non A/C 3: Semi Deluxe 4: Four Bed 5: Economy Default: 1
Name	Name	String	False	Format: Text Maximum length: 100

Bill entity data model

We have used the Invoice entity to store bill information for the customer. We have created and customized the following Invoice entity fields:

Field name	Display name	Type	Custom attribute	Comments
new_NetTotal	Net Total	Money	True	Minimum value: 0 Maximum value: 1000000000 Precision: 4
new_FoodCost	Food Cost	Money	True	Minimum value: 0 Maximum value: 1000000000 Precision: 4

Field name	Display name	Type	Custom attribute	Comments
TotalLineItemAmount	Total Room Rent	Money	False	Minimum value: -922337203685477
				Maximum value: 922337203685477
				Precision: 2

Index

M

Thank you for buying
Microsoft Dynamics CRM 2011 Application Design

About Packt Publishing

Packt, pronounced 'packed', published its first book "Mastering phpMyAdmin for Effective MySQL Management" in April 2004 and subsequently continued to specialize in publishing highly focused books on specific technologies and solutions.

Our books and publications share the experiences of your fellow IT professionals in adapting and customizing today's systems, applications, and frameworks. Our solution based books give you the knowledge and power to customize the software and technologies you're using to get the job done. Packt books are more specific and less general than the IT books you have seen in the past. Our unique business model allows us to bring you more focused information, giving you more of what you need to know, and less of what you don't.

Packt is a modern, yet unique publishing company, which focuses on producing quality, cutting-edge books for communities of developers, administrators, and newbies alike. For more information, please visit our website: www.packtpub.com.

About Packt Enterprise

In 2010, Packt launched two new brands, Packt Enterprise and Packt Open Source, in order to continue its focus on specialization. This book is part of the Packt Enterprise brand, home to books published on enterprise software – software created by major vendors, including (but not limited to) IBM, Microsoft and Oracle, often for use in other corporations. Its titles will offer information relevant to a range of users of this software, including administrators, developers, architects, and end users.

Writing for Packt

We welcome all inquiries from people who are interested in authoring. Book proposals should be sent to author@packtpub.com. If your book idea is still at an early stage and you would like to discuss it first before writing a formal book proposal, contact us; one of our commissioning editors will get in touch with you.

We're not just looking for published authors; if you have strong technical skills but no writing experience, our experienced editors can help you develop a writing career, or simply get some additional reward for your expertise.

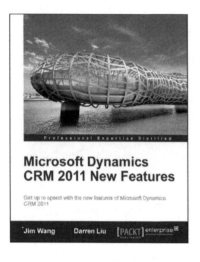

Microsoft Dynamics CRM 2011 New Features

ISBN: 978-1-849682-06-0   Paperback: 288 pages

Get up to speed with the new features of Microsoft Dynamics CRM 2011

1. Master the new features of Microsoft Dynamics 2011

2. Use client-side programming to perform data validation, automation, and process enhancement

3. Learn powerful event driven server-side programming methods: Plug-Ins and Processes (Formerly Workflows)

Microsoft Dynamics CRM 2011: Dashboards Cookbook

ISBN: 978-1-849684-40-8   Paperback: 266 pages

Over 50 simple but incredibly effective recipes for creating, customizing, and interacting with rich dashboards and charts

1. Take advantage of all of the latest Dynamics CRM dashboard features for visualizing your most important data at a glance.

2. Understand how iFrames, chart customizations, advanced WebResources and more can improve your dashboards in Dynamics CRM by using this book and eBook.

3. A highly practical cookbook bursting with a range of exciting task-based recipes for mastering Microsoft Dynamics CRM 2011 Dashboards.

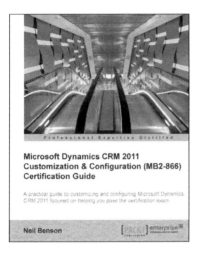

Microsoft Dynamics CRM 2011 Customization & Configuration (MB2-866) Certification Guide

ISBN: 978-1-849685-801   Paperback: 345 pages

A practical guide to customizing and configuring Microsoft Dynamics CRM 2011 focused on helping you pass the certification exam

1. Based on the official syllabus for course 80294B to help prepare you for the MB2-866 exam

2. Filled with all the procedures you need to know to pass the exam including screenshots

3. Take the practice exam with 75 sample questions to assess your knowledge before you sit the real exam

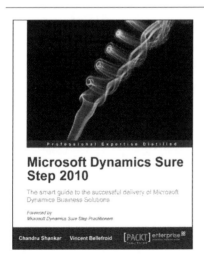

Microsoft Dynamics Sure Step 2010

ISBN: 978-1-849681-10-0   Paperback: 360 pages

The smart guide to the successful delivery of Microsoft Dynamics Business Solutions

1. Learn how to effectively use Microsoft Dynamics Sure Step to implement the right Dynamics business solution with quality, on-time and on-budget results.

2. Gain knowledge of the project and change management content provided in Microsoft Dynamics Sure Step.

3. Familiarize yourself with the approach to adopting the Microsoft Dynamics Sure Step methodology as your own.

Please check **www.PacktPub.com** for information on our titles

22075219R00134